Forever Young

Forever Young:
A Ghetto Story

Darrah Teitel

SCIROCCO DRAMA

Forever Young: A Ghetto Story
first published 2024 by Scirocco Drama
An imprint of J. Gordon Shillingford Publishing Inc.
© 2024 Darrah Teitel

Excerpt from *Five Cities of Refuge: Weekly Reflections on Genesis, Exodus, Leviticus, Numbers, and Deuteronomy* by Lawrence Kushner and David Mamet, copyright © 2003 by Rabbi Lawrence Kushner and David Mamet. Used by permission of Schocken Books, an imprint of the Knopf Doubleday Publishing Group, a division of Penguin Random House LLC. All rights reserved.

Scirocco Drama Editor: Glenda MacFarlane
Cover design by Doowah Design
Author photo by Dahlia Katz
Production photos by Curtis Perry

Printed and bound in Canada on 100% post-consumer recycled paper.
We acknowledge the financial support of the Manitoba Arts Council and
The Canada Council for the Arts for our publishing program.

Production inquiries to:
Ian Arnold, Artist's Representative
PO Box 98074
RPO Queen and Carlaw
Toronto, Ontario, Canada M4M 3L9
ian@catalysttcm.com
www.catalysttcm.com
+01-416-568-8673

Library and Archives Canada Cataloguing in Publication

Title: Forever young : a ghetto story / Darrah Teitel.
Names: Teitel, Darrah, author.
Identifiers: Canadiana 20240358066 | ISBN 9781990738364 (softcover)
Subjects: LCGFT: Drama.
Classification: LCC PS8639.E38 F67 2024 | DDC C812/.6—dc23

J. Gordon Shillingford Publishing
P.O. Box 86, RPO Corydon Avenue, Winnipeg, MB Canada R3M 3S3

*When I was in Grade Six my parents would huddle in fear
every night, afraid to answer the phone lest it be yet another
one of my teachers complaining about me.*

*During this period, one teacher gave me unqualified support
and encouragement. She handed back one of my assignments
with the following note: "Darrah, when you publish your
first book, please dedicate it to me, your teacher,
who so enjoyed reading your work."*

Those words have stayed with me over the years.

*So, partner, children, parents and grandparents, you will
have to wait your turns. This book is dedicated with love and
gratitude to my Grade Six English teacher, Donnie Friedman.*

Praise for *Forever Young: A Ghetto Story*

"For readers outside the Jewish community, every line of this play will launch you into a vibrant, surprising and delicious world of contradiction, passion and debate. Since October 2023, the Jewish world has been fractured by questions of genocide, apartheid, ethno-nationalism and more. For anyone confused about the roots of this debate, Forever Young is the community context note for the state of Jewishness today."

—Avi Lewis and Naomi Klein

"Terrific cast and plot propel *Forever Young*. It's a heavy topic, to be sure, but playwright Darrah Teitel balances the bleak outlook with a welcome touch of humour, most evident in the relationships between the characters....it's a piece that achieves the challenging task of bringing a dark chapter of Holocaust history into the light in a way that not only illustrates the humanity of the oppressed and, lest we forget, the Nazis' extraordinary capacity for evil, but also connects with contemporary audiences..."

—Lynn Saxberg, *Ottawa Citizen*

"LGBT+ relationships are not often portrayed in historical fiction, but this play accentuated the importance of intertwining the past with the present to normalize LGBT+ stories within historical contexts...... In a time when LGBT+ relationships and strong female characters were not at the forefront of historical accounts, the play shed light on the value of these important historical perspectives."

—Audrey Gunn, *The Charlatan*

"*Forever Young: A Ghetto Story* is a play that fictionalizes what a group of young people might have gone through on the eve of mass deportation from the Warsaw Ghetto to the Treblinka death camp. Believe it or not, this play is also a comedy. It finds laughter, entertainment, hope and humanity in the darkest of times. But it is also a reminder that resistance to fascism and oppression can and should lead to a questioning of capitalist society itself."

—Chantal Sundaram, *Socialist Worker*

Darrah Teitel

Darrah Teitel is a playwright and socialist living in Toronto where she currently works as a labour organizer. She is a graduate of The National Theatre School of Canada's Playwriting program. Her most recent credits include *Forever Young* (Great Canadian Theatre Company 2022), *The Omnibus Bill* (Counterpoint Players 2019), *Behaviour* (Great Canadian Theatre Company / SpiderWebShow 2019), *Corpus* (Teesri Duniya and Counterpoint Players 2014), and *The Apology* (Alberta Theatre Projects 2013).

Darrah is the winner of several awards for her plays and has been nominated for Dora, META, Betty Mitchell and Prix Rideau awards for best new play. She was a member of the 2007, 2011, and 2012 Banff Playwright's Colony, The MacDowell Colony, The Gros Morne Playwrights Residency and the Asylum Arts Peleh Family Artists Residency in Berkeley, California.

Acknowledgements

Forever Young was written in the first year of the Covid-19 pandemic, in the months right after my second child was born. It would not have been possible without generous support from Asylum Arts and the Peleh Family International Artists Residency which brought my entire family to live in Berkeley, California so I could write this play. There, I benefited hugely from dramaturgical, intellectual, near-spiritual support from Dan Schifrin and Josh Kornbluth. Thank you to that whole team, especially Rebecca Guber, Jane Gottesman and Geoffrey Biddle.

Thanks to Tamar Szmuilowicz for giving me her copy of *The Ghetto Fights*, Illya Mykytyn for the Polish, Adam Nayman for the generative chats, Rabbi Elizabeth Bolton for her chaplaincy, Jonathan Garfinkle for his counsel when the play was under attack, and Sarah Kitz and Evan Webber for their obvious ongoing contributions to the play and my life. Thanks to my many brothers and sisters and comrades under whose scrutiny and solidarity I get to call myself a socialist.

Thank you to my parents, Linda Speigel and Murray Teitel and to all four of my grandparents without whose voices and influence I would have little to write about.

Thank you to my partner, Sebastian Ronderos-Morgan, who moved across the continent to care for our kids, one a newborn, while their Mama wrote this play. I couldn't keep doing this art thing without your support and our constant conversation.

Director's Note

Frequently we approach Holocaust narratives with a particular set of expectations.

Darrah and I were determined not to meet them.

Firstly, the play is full of humour. One of Darrah Teitel's greatest gifts is her ability to write comedy into situations where laughter would seem impossible. Secondly, this show does not meet the requirements of a historically loyal period piece, as you will see. We broke with historical loyalty on purpose: it was our intent to delve into this particular moment in history, and these people, while allowing the story to exceed its frame.

Forever Young is a story of brave youth pushing against the status quo under dire circumstances to address their survival. It is very much about a specific moment in history, and it is about now.

The characters are messy, awkward and flawed. They are human, not storybook heroes, as a backward glance through history might cast them. These kids — sometimes unkind, unreasonable, deeply loving, uncertain, overly certain — try and fail. What they are able to enact in their brief time together is a dream of solidarity and collaboration across ideological lines towards the creation of a better world.

The knowledge of how to do this accrues and is passed from one generation to another. We must claim these incremental victories. They are part of the memory and knowledge of the world. They light the path forward.

Sarah Kitz
5784
2023

Sarah Kitz is the artistic director of Ottawa's Great Canadian Theatre Company. She directed the premiere production of Forever Young.

Foreword

How is a play like a human being? I've been thinking about this
question since last Saturday, sitting at the table with Darrah, she
across from me under the lamp in the living room. We'd decided
on a few days of meetings to talk about her last adjustments to
Forever Young: A Ghetto Story and for me to write this foreword.
Saturday was the day we'd chosen to begin. Saturday also
turned out to be the day Hamas launched its stupefying attack
on Israel from Gaza. In the few days since (it's Wednesday
now), thousands have been killed, and Israel has declared war.
Yoav Gallant, Israel's Defense Minister, has announced a "total
siege" of Gaza, portending suffering and destruction beyond
what was already beyond imagining. "We are fighting human
animals," said Gallant, "and we must act accordingly."

When I read those words of Gallant's, I felt like I was seeing
them written in chalk, like they were on a blackboard in some
original cosmic schoolhouse of misery. I needed to look out
the window. That's when I noticed it, my question, while I
was looking away from the words in chalk. How is a play like
a human being? Which I think means: how is a proposal for
action—a play, a publication, a set of documents, perhaps even
a declaration of war—like or unlike its author? What part of
the proposal must be a repetition and what part of it might one
hope not to recognize, to encounter as something new? Does it
possess some kind of humanity?

It is certainly foolish to ask such a large question in an
introductory note that has to be sent to the publisher today
(it's already late, in fact). But I think I am also required to ask
because this play is asking this question, too. It asks, I think, in

the particular way that it presents its *Ghetto Story*. The ghetto in the play is called the Warsaw Ghetto, but it's other ghettos too, including the ghetto of politics. In all of these places, stories are the materials that give or fail to give people leverage—choices about how our proposals may or may not be reflexive repetitions. How is a play like a human being?

***

On the ground level of fiction, *Forever Young* is about survival. It's one group versus another—good kids, bad Nazis. But the Nazis here are ambient—the clock of the final solution just ticks away in the background. What we see instead are the kids, riven by political differences that may not be reconcilable. The outcome, their survival, hinges on whether solidarity between the different splinters of Polish socialism is possible: can the ethnocultural and internationalist factions (not to mention the capitalists) pull together in time to organize and fight back? The teenaged avatars of these factions, even without the benefit of historical hindsight, are not at all certain they can pull it off. They try, by turns, to defend themselves, to live in a kind of togetherness, and finally, to record their lives and preserve the documents of their political efforts. They seek to gain entrance to the Archive, which they conceptualize as a repository of revolutionary energy for the future.

The narrative structure is that of a tragedy, but the play is ultimately ambivalent about what its tragedy *is*. Is it the mass death of the Holocaust itself or the class war that it enflamed to violence between its victims? Is it the "necessary" betrayal of the Ghetto fighters by the Polish Socialist Party during the Ghetto Uprising? Or is it the Soviet betrayal of the Poles during the Warsaw Uprising? Or perhaps most trickily: is the tragedy the death of a bunch of imaginary teenaged socialists? Or is it the death of a bunch of imaginary teenaged *Jews*?

All of this ambivalence about tragedy has the effect of placing *Forever Young* at a critical remove from the genre of Holocaust fiction. The tropes of Holocaust fiction are both the target and aesthetic point of origin for *Forever Young*. I am gratified by the middle finger that the play raises to Shoah kitsch. But maintaining that stance would be too easy—read: moralistic. The real subject is the rhetorical power of sentimentalized suffering.

I am destabilized—and I mean that as praise—at how the play appraises the *usefulness* of the victim's status. What's disturbing about that look is the admission it makes that there's no such thing as a clean fight, especially when the fight's with one's own family. The conclusion of that thought is something like Heiner Müller's statement, that "The model for this century and for its principle of selection" is Auschwitz; that "The problem with this civilization is that it does not have an alternative to Auschwitz," only different strategies for selection, different ways to feign one's surprise about where and why the selection occurs.

That is, indeed, the frame of our political experience, perhaps today, especially. Not a pretty picture. Nonetheless, even from inside, there can be events, surprises that break the frame (and suddenly alongside the sentence comes Paul Celan, saying that a poem doesn't reach outside or above time *but through—through*).

To me there is the possibility, in *Forever Young*, of such a surprise. It hinges on a simple question of documentation. The play is based on documentary evidence—Marek Edelmen's *The Ghetto Fights* being the key text. But the paucity of historical archival material connected to the young fighters of the Warsaw Ghetto, to their anti-capitalist practice in particular, means that basically everything, right up to the characters' names, has been made up. All we know is that there were people like this who lived. As such, the play's core pretense is both absurd and plausible: it gets to be both a fiction and also the authentic completion of a documentary effort.

This position is contradictory. The author's words, the performers' efforts at listening and articulation, the audience's attention and breath, cannot reveal the facts, but only the edges of the contradiction. The performance of Jewish identity also falls, will fall, into this field. Far from being failures, these encounters with the limits of knowledge and imagination—

the play's determined unfinishedness—reveal and exercise a tolerance for complexity. One might call this tolerance resilience. Whatever it is, it's something we need, whether we're human beings or human animals, if we intend to create livable worlds.

I was sick with Covid when this play was first produced in 2022. I was miserable, but for the sake of this text, my absence was fortunate, because my recollection is limited to the first days of the company's staging. The start of rehearsal sometimes reveals both what's possible and what's essential about a play—particularly with a sensitive and courageous director leading the research. Those days' experience aligns with what I believed before and believe still, here at the table, under the lamp: that what's essential is this play's unfinishedness. It must be found and be cared for; it must be kept open so as to make space for its own undertaking. (That must be the case of every play that has merit—the trick being to make the unfinishedness particular, precise and distinct.)

How is a play like a human being? It must be something to do with the body. And also *not* the body.

I think of burial. In Jewish tradition, the bereaved don't leave the side of the grave without shovelling dirt on the coffin. In this way you participate in the dead's swallowing up. The action of covering over becomes your action, combines both the memory of the dead and the memory of you going on after it. Burial may be the best analogy I can think of for this play, and the open grave itself the unfinishedness that somehow will become new ground. There it is, and here we are.

Evan Webber
October 2023

Evan Webber is a writer and performance maker. He lives in Toronto. He was the dramaturg for the premiere production of Forever Young.

Production History

Forever Young: A Ghetto Story premiered at Great Canadian Theatre Company in Ottawa, Ontario, November 8–20, 2022, with the following cast and creative team:

Aviva Armour-Ostroff:............................... Felicia

Ori Black: .... Izzy

Brittany Kay: ....Eden

Drew Moore:.................................... Christian

Billie Nell: ....Joshua

Laurie Champagne:............................ Stage Manager

Olivier Fairfield:................................. Sound Designer

Seth Gerry:..Lighting Designer

Vanessa Imeson:............................Costume Designer

Sarah Kitz:... Director

Jane Osborn: .... Assistant Stage Manager

Megan Piercey Monafu:.................. Intimacy Director

Brian Smith:............................... Set Designer

Darrah Teitel:................................Playwright

Evan Webber: ....Dramaturg

Billie Nell, Aviva Armour-Ostroff, Drew Moore, Ori Black and Brittany Kay in the GCTC production of *Forever Young*, 2022, directed by Sarah Kitz. Photo by Curtis Perry.

Billie Nell, Ori Black and Brittany Kay in the Great Canadian Theatre Company production of *Forever Young*, 2022, directed by Sarah Kitz. Photo by Curtis Perry.

Brittany Kay and Ori Black in the Great Canadian Theatre Company production of *Forever Young*, 2022, directed by Sarah Kitz. Photo by Curtis Perry.

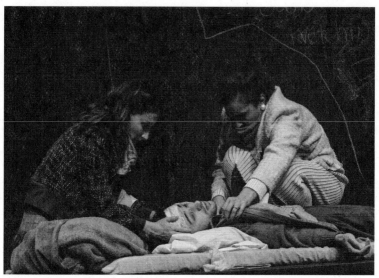

Brittany Kay, Ori Black, and Aviva Armour-Ostroff in the Great Canadian Theatre Company production of *Forever Young*, 2022, directed by Sarah Kitz. Photo by Curtis Perry.

Brittany Kay, Ori Black, and Billie Nell in the Great Canadian
Theatre Company production of *Forever Young*, 2022, directed by
Sarah Kitz. Photo by Curtis Perry.

Drew Moore and Brittany Kay in the Great Canadian Theatre
Company production of *Forever Young*, 2022, directed by Sarah Kitz.
Photo by Curtis Perry.

Ori Black and Brittany Kay in the Great Canadian Theatre Company production of *Forever Young*, 2022, directed by Sarah Kitz. Photo by Curtis Perry.

Ori Black in the Great Canadian Theatre Company production of *Forever Young*, 2022, directed by Sarah Kitz. Photo by Curtis Perry.

Characters

Felicia Czerniakow:	Middle-aged. The wife of Adam Czerniakow, the Chairman of the Judenrat (Jewish Council).
Izzy (Isador) Chaim:	Nineteen. A Bund Party member.
Eden Abromavitch:	Nineteen. A Bund Party member.
Christian Dobrowski:	Early Twenties. A Polish Socialist Party member.
Joshua Liebskind:	Seventeen. A Hashomer Hatzair Movement member.

Togetherness

*The actors who are playing the characters
set up the stage while the audience settles.
The song "Forever Young" by Alphaville
plays while they do this, and the actors
can enjoy the music while the house lights
change and focus is brought to the stage.
At around this point, one of the actors can
cue the stage manager to play a recording
of the story by Rabbi Kushner featured on
the previous page.*

In *Five Cities of Refuge*, Rabbi Lawrence Kushner writes:

"So, the Israelites follow Moses and his God only to wind up
between the approaching Egyptian chariots and the abyss of
the Red Sea. Now there is no turning back, no moving forward.

It is logically impossible; cannot be done. You can either be
'in the midst of the sea,' or you can be 'on dry ground.' But
you cannot, at the same time, be both. The Hasidic master
Dov Baer of Mezritch teaches that there is a place, an order of
being, called *Ayin*, Nothingness, through which anyone (or
anything) must pass before it can become something new. Just
a split second after it is no longer what it was but before it is
what it would become. This is a place of great terror. When you
enter the Nothingness, there can be no guarantees. All bets are
off. You could become anything — or remain nothing, forever.
Such a place contains both a thing *and* its opposite: Sea *and* dry
ground. Life *and* death. Good *and* evil. Slavery *and* freedom.

You want to know what happened at the sea? I'll tell you. The waters didn't literally split. The people all walked into the sea and drowned. Then they all walked up onto the opposite shore, reborn into free men and women. Into the *Ayin*..."

ACTOR
PLAYING IZZY: So, it's July 1942. Okay?

> *It is an old theatre—once vaudeville, then movie, then cabaret, now abandoned. In the room are a mimeograph machine, several typewriters and a single bed with a curtain rigged up around it, like a shower curtain. Papers are stacked everywhere. IZZY is terrified.*

IZZY: *(Sings to calm himself.)*
Oh rise, ye prisoners of starvation
Arise, ye wretched of the earth.
For justice thunders condemnation
A better world's in birth!

> *JOSHUA enters.*

JOSHUA: Izzy?

> *Sees him.*

Do you have the witness statement?

IZZY: Sing with me, boychick.

Oh rise, ye prisoners of starvation!
Arise, ye wretched of the earth!

JOSHUA: You sing *Oh rise* in the first line and then arise in the second?

IZZY: Yes!

JOSHUA: It's chaotic. Arise is correct.

IZZY: *Arise... Oh rise!* Yes, I have the witness statement.

JOSHUA: You should be quiet.

IZZY: Singing is good for the nervous system. You
                 need to feel strong? *(Throws a fierce arm around
                 him.)* Sing, Joshy.

                         JOSHUA sings with him.

                 So, comrades, come rally
                 To the last fight we will face
                 The Internationale will unite the human race!

IZZY: Yes! Joshua, my love, this is why I love you.

                 You have a brain like a robot, but you sing
                 so sweet. We'll print the eyewitness. Eden
                 Abromavitch comes. We sleep.

JOSHUA: Eden Abromavitch is still coming tonight?

IZZY: Yes.

JOSHUA: Oh.

IZZY: Don't be jealous.

JOSHUA: I'm not jealous. I'm afraid.

IZZY: Joshy... You feel afraid, but you stay put.
                 That's / why I love you.

JOSHUA: / why you love me.

IZZY: Yes.

                         Kisses JOSHUA on the mouth.

JOSHUA: There are tears on your cheeks.

                         *IZZY produces the eyewitness statement
                         for JOSHUA to see. It is a carefully
                         concealed onionskin scroll.*

                 Want to see it? This thing from the witness?

> *IZZY lays out the onion skin scroll on a table.*
>
> You read it, boychick. My eyes are getting old.

JOSHUA: You're nineteen.

IZZY: I'm a hundred and twenty years old. A fucking patriarch.

JOSHUA: "This is the true and unmolested eyewitness account of two committed members of the Bund and Polish Socialist Parties, respectively, Warsaw Chapters. We do hereby attest that after having faithfully followed a transport of approximately six hundred Jewish men, women and children from Warsaw to Treblinka on July 26, 1942. Comrade Grabowski of the Polish Communist Party a rail line worker and member of union Local 37 enabled Comrade Zalman Zygmunt of the Bund to follow the rail transport of cattle cars—"

IZZY: Sha! Don't read aloud. These words are a fucking curse.

> *JOSHUA reads in his head.*
>
> Do you know what Mark Twain said? Do you know this Mark Twain? Do you read novels?

JOSHUA: American, 1835 to 1910? No, I don't.

IZZY: "You should because this Twain said: The difference between fiction and reality is that the former must lie within the boundaries of the possible." You get it? Fiction is boring: it's all the ways they've killed us already, but we couldn't have imagined gas. Not before now."

JOSHUA: *(Finishes reading.)* Gas... Sometimes they've used gas.

IZZY: Not in trucks. In *rooms*, he says. Big buildings. Hundreds of yids in, hundreds of yid bodies out.

JOSHUA: No. Thousands. Maybe tens of thousands?

IZZY: And don't ask me where my family is, Liebskind. Just please don't ask. It makes a boy want to believe in the bullshit. They're at work camp! They're building planes in Siberia! *(IZZY screams.)* Ahhhhhhhhh!

JOSHUA: *Sha!* Please. We need to print it immediately. Schulich wants me to report back when it's done. Here, he sent you orders.

IZZY: These Brushmaker cell machers... He thinks he's my cell captain.

JOSHUA: He is your cell captain.

IZZY: Ahhh, but who has the plan and the connections to collude with the PPS to smuggle guns and gasoline and whole women into our ranks? Me!

JOSHUA: He doesn't think Eden Abromavitch is actually coming. He wants me to report back if she comes after we print the pamphlets.

IZZY: Feh! *(Takes note.)* It says he thinks she's nuts for wanting to live here. That she's my responsibility if she's nuts and I'm to keep her with me. They send me orders stating the obvious... I hope you didn't risk your life to convey this redundant information... What time is it?

JOSHUA: Three minutes to the hour. I didn't.

IZZY: Who will Joshua be without his watch?

JOSHUA: No, I need my watch.

IZZY: You need to sell it.

JOSHUA: I will.

IZZY: Before it's worthless. She's coming in three minutes.

JOSHUA: But Izzy? Why are you smuggling whole women into the Ghetto?

IZZY: It's Eden. You'll see. Eden isn't just any comrade.

JOSHUA: Oh.

IZZY: She's formidable. Don't be—

JOSHUA: I'm not!

IZZY: Also she's sleeping with the Youth President of the Warsaw Polish Socialist Party, so it doesn't hurt to have her here with us, nu?

JOSHUA: Oh.

IZZY: Oh, he says… Listen, when she comes, you go away for a bit. I want to be alone with her for a little.

JOSHUA: Why? How long?

IZZY: Come here. *(Tries to hold him.)*

JOSHUA: No…

IZZY: Yes. *(They kiss.)* There just isn't a lot of time left, so we might need to overlap a bit with our affections. Okay, sweetness?

JOSHUA: I can't leave with the shooting.

IZZY: *(Finds a spot for him.)* How about here?

JOSHUA: Okay. I'll hide. You won't notice me.

IZZY: I do notice you. But this is a really big room.
             Look! And read it again, Joshy… It's reality
             now.

             *From off, EDEN rises and tries to figure out
             how to send a code into the scene. She tries
             stomping and whistling. She can't whistle.
             She tasks the actor playing CHRISTIAN
             to whistle for her. It's awkward. IZZY
             whistles back. JOSHUA takes the gas lamp,
             the onionskin and some paper to write
             on into the corner of the room where he
             becomes inconspicuous behind a curtain.
             EDEN is breathless and also nineteen. She
             takes a tepid step into the room as a shaft of
             light pours in from the hallway.*

IZZY: Welcome to the Ghetto, girlchick.

EDEN: Isador? Izzy? Thank you, God!

IZZY: Well, it's not God's doing…

EDEN: I thought, this is a trap.

IZZY: But you're welcome.

EDEN: Every step, I thought this is it.

IZZY: You're too beautiful to shoot in the street.

EDEN: You're flirting with me?

IZZY: Good we got you through—we've only used
             that route for potatoes, never girls.

             EDEN punches his arm.

             What? Potato is life!

EDEN: Still a total schmuck.

             *They embrace. There's an awkward bulge
             under EDEN's coat.*

IZZY: Woah…

EDEN: Relax, it's a plant.

IZZY: You bring a plant? Is it even edible?

EDEN: Don't touch it. You know that we all think you're dead out there.

IZZY: Nope. To everyone's great annoyance, I live…They know I'm here, too, these goyishe communists… Did they actually say I was dead?

EDEN: Isn't everyone dead?

IZZY: The Bund is alive and thriving!

EDEN;   I need to sit.

IZZY: Well, some of us are dead. Even dead, we're thriving!

EDEN: Can I sit down for a minute?

She collapses slightly.

IZZY: It's your adrenaline that keeps you steady when you think you're in danger. Now you feel safe, the fear is going to flood in. Run—don't think. Pause—shit your pants.

EDEN: Did you get into medical school? I forget.

IZZY: Almost! I got a whole war to study for the next exam. You're also going to feel hungry in a minute. Here.

Passes her some bread.

EDEN: Your mother will shep more nachas from a famous doctor than a famous radical. How are they?

IZZY: Who?

EDEN: Your family.

         IZZY doesn't answer.

         Oy… Where are they?

IZZY: Unclear. And your parents? They…

EDEN: We hid separate. I haven't heard a single thing. They're not here, then?

IZZY: No.

EDEN: Maybe you didn't see them?

IZZY: It's only a few kilometres—we know who's here. So they're safe. Probably safe.

EDEN: I wanted to stay working on the outside. I thought, they can't just round me up and force me to stop, and who could tell how long this would go on or how big the Ghetto would grow. And what? You knew. Somehow you knew it was going to get this bad.

IZZY: I'm good at worst case scenarios. Speaking of which, how's Christian?

EDEN: Fine.

IZZY: You've been hiding with him.

EDEN: With the Party. The Polish Socialist Party that you and I are both active members of. They offered to hide me.

IZZY: Christian Dabrowski offered. In his mother's cellar.

EDEN: His mother is a good woman.

IZZY: Until she needed you gone. She kicked you out.

EDEN:	I was going to get Christian's family killed. So, I told the PPS to ask you—
IZZY:	Me? You thought I was dead, you said.
EDEN:	Okay—fine. I knew you weren't dead.
IZZY:	I knew that you knew. You wanted to be assigned to my cell.
EDEN:	Who told you that?
IZZY:	Dabrowski, naturally. Why do you lie?
EDEN:	Because you're making my cheeks burn, you're so arrogant!
IZZY:	It's okay that we should want to be together. *(He touches her.)* We missed each other.
EDEN:	I was going crazy in that cellar. What mishugaas to sit in a cellar while my comrades are organizing to fight in here?
IZZY:	With the rats and the typhus?
EDEN:	You have typhus? You look okay to me.
IZZY:	I do look good, don't I? How's Dabrowski look these days? Blonder?
EDEN:	He's ginger. You know that. And he looks worse than you—with all your rats and typhus.
IZZY:	Like every good plague, the typhus is killing the poorest first, and my family has money. Had money. I have some money…anyhow, the starvelings have lice and typhus. Don't touch them. The rich are being bled more slowly and with connections to the black market some of them do a good business, but don't touch them either, you'll catch false consciousness. They sit in cafes, each of these

insipid petite bourgeoisie feeling like the single most persecuted person on the planet. They kvetch about their oppression then step right over a child with a bloated belly on the street. Even the Nazis haven't killed the curse of capitalism in Jewish Warsaw. Course, they did start killing the capitalists, recently... So... *(He gives a thumbs up.)*

EDEN: It's good to see you again, Isador.

IZZY: You too, Comrade, it's good to see you too.

EDEN: Izzy?

IZZY: Ya.

EDEN: Where do you think my parents are?

IZZY: Come here.

> *She comes for a hug. He kisses her. She shoves him hard.*

EDEN: Izzy! What?

IZZY: What? No?

EDEN: No!

IZZY: Why no?

EDEN: You need more than no? You knucked my teeth!

IZZY: Okay, okay... Not yet.

EDEN: Yet? You want to feel what you did to my teeth?

> *EDEN tries to punch his face. He feints.*

IZZY: I thought we agreed not now!

EDEN: You're such an idiot! I want to leave.

IZZY: You can't leave, or did you forget you're a Jew again.?

EDEN: You think I don't know I'm Jewish?

IZZY: There's Jewish in a cellar and Jewish in a cage, girlchick.

EDEN: I didn't like your "girlchick" in high school and I don't like it now.

IZZY: Yes, you did. Sit down, Comrade Abromavitch. Listen. *(Shots can be heard.)* This is where you are. It's a cage.

EDEN: You're the cage!

IZZY: I'm your cell captain. Here's your ration book, *(Reads.)* Zehava Altberg, may her memory be a blessing.

EDEN: Where do I sleep? In this movie theatre?

IZZY: Don't offend her! She's a cabaret! But no, you sleep with me in a flat.

EDEN: With you?

IZZY: Don't get too excited. We share one bedroom with two other families, and we move every two weeks to keep ahead of arrests. This is the third of four organized Ghetto quadrants and we do the printing.

EDEN: You remember what I did in the Bund, right? I'm an organizer. I'm not just here to copy edit.

IZZY: You want to fight?

EDEN: Yes, *Captain!*

IZZY: Oh, I like Captain... Teach the other girls to say it like that.

> *JOSHUA clears his throat and steps out of the shadow. EDEN screams. JOSHUA bows politely.*

EDEN: Gotenyu!

JOSHUA: Pardon me for interrupting. I could see he had no intention of letting you know I am here. Here I am!

IZZY: Comrade Eden Abromavitch, this is Comrade Joshua Liebskind.

JOSHUA: A pleasure and an honour to meet a legendary Bund comrade.

IZZY: Joshy is sixteen.

EDEN: A pleasure to meet you too, Comrade.

JOSHUA: I'm actually not a Bund Party member. I'm the Warsaw chapter chairman for Hashomer Hatzair. And I'm *seventeen*. And now we need to get to work.

IZZY: Not a Bundist—a Zionist. He's not a real socialist because he's too sentimental and unrealistic.

JOSHUA: He means that I'm going to Palestine.

IZZY: Should have gone already but he was too young.

JOSHUA: My family needs me.

IZZY: To stay home because he is so young.

EDEN: That's great, Comrade. I was going to join Hashomer too, at one point. I greatly respect your movement.

IZZY: Except that she doesn't, and she thinks that Zionists are idiots. And anyway, now that we've met, it's time to do the work. But first, just answer me one question: *why the fuck* would we create an ethnic nationalist war in Palestine when that is literally what is killing us here in Poland? And imagine the hair? A bunch of Pollack Yids walking around Arabia with our hair! She irons her hair! Back when she had an iron, that's what she did!

EDEN: When do you stop? Does he ever stop?

JOSHUA: He stops at nine twenty-five in the morning, when he must relinquish the meeting room to me for the nine-thirty chapter meeting for Hashomer. Then he goes to work in the co-operative barber shop until seven p.m. After that we do the printing. That's what we need to do now. Every Thursday at five a.m. we train with weapons.

IZZY: Isn't he cute?

EDEN: You're rude.

IZZY: He likes it when I tease him.

JOSHUA: He likes to think I like it. In fact, I just don't care.

IZZY: It doesn't bother him. He's a pacifist.

EDEN: A pacifist?

JOSHUA: I'm training in the dialectical art of non-violent communication.

IZZY: Luckily, the other Hashomer kids want to fight. Look.

IZZY reveals the supplies he uses to make petrol bombs from bottles, kerosene, sand and rags.

EDEN: Oh my god…

IZZY: Don't touch!

JOSHUA: There's no time for this. It's ten twenty-six now, which means we have just under twelve hours to get the eyewitness pamphlet out. I copied it.

EDEN: What eyewitness?

JOSHUA: This—

IZZY: Joshua!

JOSHUA: What?

IZZY: She doesn't know anything yet, Joshua, are you dumb?

EDEN: Know what?

               EDEN grabs the pamphlet.

JOSHUA: I'm not dumb!

               EDEN is reading.

IZZY: Okay! Well…

JOSHUA: I'm not dumb, Izzy. Don't say that.

               IZZY brings three chairs together for them all to sit while EDEN reads the eyewitness statement.

IZZY: I'm sorry. This is the reality now, girlchick.

The Warsaw Ghetto

While these interstitial texts are spoken by some combination of the actors, they record and transcribe the information in writing, pictures, and drawing in a way that is visible to the audience. In the premiere production, the actors drew on the walls of the stage in chalk, as a teacher might in a classroom, but the choice of how to capture the words for the audience in subsequent productions may vary.

The Warsaw Ghetto was about three square kilometres and at its height, early in the occupation of Warsaw, it imprisoned more than 500,000 Jews, who were variously being starved, arrested, shot on the street, and killed by disease. The wide part of the Ghetto was pretty much from Somerset to the Queensway. So like the size of Centretown with a little gerrymandered tail to include some of the Glebe.[1]

Warsaw before the 1939 was one of those exciting, thriving, multicultural cities, not unlike this one. One full third of the city was Jewish, which is very unlike this one. Israel is the only place where there are cities with that many Jews per capita today.

Ghetto Society

There were all kinds of Jews: religious, secular, rich, poor, socialist, communist, liberal-capitalist, Zionist and anti-Zionist. And within those categories there was huge

---

[1] *Change this section so that it is specific to whichever city the play is being performed in.*

diversity. There were ten kinds of Orthodox Jews and some were Zionist and some weren't, and four kinds of socialist, and some were secular and some weren't and some followed Trotsky and some didn't. The Ghetto was an open-air prison. Trapped inside the Ghetto, the Jews didn't become one people. Instead, all their social divisions redoubled; people mistrusted one another and fought and kvetched.

And above them all—acting as a puppet government under the occupation and enslavement—was the Jewish Council, the Judenrat. They were instrumental in assisting the SS and establishing the Jewish Police who helped to manage the Genocide. The question of whether the Judenrat could have disobeyed the Nazi occupation is a matter of great controversy.

Ghetto Life

The last scene happened in July 1942; seven weeks later the Ghetto sustained a massive wave of deportations. About 200,000 of the 500,000 people were either killed in the streets of the Ghetto or taken by train to Treblinka. After these events, the Ghetto returned to a relative state of calm that was nonetheless very fucking bad.

It can be hard to imagine the situation of the Warsaw Ghetto, but the difficulty is lessened by the fact that similar Ghettoes exist today—open-air prisons for people who are considered undesirable or inconvenient to the local ruling class.

Certain refugee camps are useful to hold in mind if one considers even the impact of how the German occupiers cut off basic supplies and building materials to the inhabitants of the Ghetto. Part of what makes things very fucking bad is not being able to get enough food or medicine or fuel for heat or supplies to repair buildings, walls and roofs.

In Continuous Session

EDEN and IZZY walk into the scene. They are in the same room, though on different sides of the curtain, so ostensibly alone. EDEN is tending her plant and a piece of the rotting ceiling literally falls off and lands dangerously close to her. EDEN screams and protectively scoops the plant up and holds it.

EDEN: Oy, shit!

IZZY rushes over to EDEN, holding a pistol.

IZZY: What happened?

EDEN: The thing! It fell on my head.

IZZY: What thing? Your head?

EDEN: Almost!

IZZY: You're fine.

EDEN: No, I'm not!

IZZY: Why are you holding the plant?

EDEN: Why are you holding a pistol?

IZZY: Put it down.

EDEN: Stop shouting at me!

IZZY: I'm not. You are.

EDEN: Everything you say to me is shouting. God!

               They put everything down.

               How can this life be so terrifying and so boring all at once?

               JOSHUA walks in to attend the meeting. He sees the hole above EDEN.

JOSHUA: I know I'm approximately seven minutes late, but you sold my watch, and also multilateral council meetings have never begun on time. The ceiling fell down? Eden, why did the ceiling fall down?

EDEN: You're blaming me?

JOSHUA: I asked a question.

EDEN: Sounds like blame.

JOSHUA: Are you angry, sad, annoyed?

EDEN: Yes. All of those things.

JOSHUA: Is there something you want to request from me?

IZZY: I do. I request you take your idiotic pacifist psychology books and burn them for fuel.

EDEN: Book. He just has one. Like a cult.

JOSHUA: Pacifism isn't a cult.

EDEN: It's worse, it's capitalism.

JOSHUA: It's communication.

EDEN: Psychology and pacifism is for rich people, who are trying to stop poor Yids from attacking their masters. Are you a rich Yid, Joshua?

JOSHUA: Can you please just help me clean up before the Chairman of the Jewish Council arrives?

EDEN: I should tidy up for a collaborator pig?

JOSHUA: It's a multilateral meeting—!

EDEN: I'd like to see him crawl through our actual shit and to come to us on his knees.

JOSHUA: Why would you treat anyone like that?

EDEN: Revenge?

JOSHUA: That is not on our list of goals for this meeting!

IZZY: Sha. Just stop.

EDEN: Why?

IZZY: Because it's starting to rain.

EDEN: Now?

JOSHUA: That's bad. Because of the hole in the ceiling.

EDEN: Okay. Don't panic. Get the mimeograph.

JOSHUA: The meeting minutes. The pamphlets— Everything paper.

IZZY: Screw the paper. My bombs!

EDEN: Oh God. He's right.

> *IZZY lunges down towards a stash of supplies for Molotov cocktails, while EDEN pulls up an area rug covering a*

hole in the floor where they keep their few weapons. JOSHUA refuses to take them and frantically gathers the papers.

IZZY: Bombs first! Joshua!

JOSHUA: When this is over, you will want the records of our fallen comrades a thousand times more than these death machines—

IZZY: Get the gasoline before I murder you.

JOSHUA: I think you're trying to be funny, but you're not funny.

EDEN: Stop it. Here. *(She hands over the last of the munitions.)* Get the minutes and the pamphlets.

The three teens rush around stuffing paper and notebooks under their shirts and then they drag chairs away from the hole in the ceiling and sit and wait for the rain.

IZZY: You know what? I don't think it's going to rain anymore.

CHRISTIAN walks in.

CHRISTIAN: Hi hi! What's everyone doing against the wall? Ooh, it's messy in here. Did we call to order yet? If you haven't, wait for a moment, because look, I brought buns! Real ones and you don't want to know what I did to get them, but then I thought—no. Christian, they should have them. Bring them to your comrades. After what happened… Is this all of you who is coming? I was expecting more. Schulich, at least, for an important meeting such as this one. A decisive meeting. I'm honoured you invited me here on behalf of the PPS.

IZZY: Schulich's gone.

CHRISTIAN: I see. So many. We heard...

IZZY: You saw, no? All the trains pulling out with people instead of cows?

CHRISTIAN: Yes. And I'm here. And so, I have bread. And... and! Even a little *butter!* See? Who wants? This is good. It will put us in the right mood to have this meeting with our bellies full. I have six. And I'll go without. I'm happy for you all to get a treat. That's satisfaction enough for me. Let's save the extra two for the Judenrat when they arrive.

                 EDEN rises holding her bloated belly of paper and waddles over to claim a bun.

EDEN: Thank you, Christian. They look delicious.

CHRISTIAN: It's real flour. *(Aside.)* Eden, thank god you are safe. I couldn't breathe.

                 A beat, as EDEN awkwardly moves over to him. She drops a leaflet.

                 What's this, you're leaking propaganda? Ha. Of course, you are.

                 EDEN lets the pamphlets fall to the floor. CHRISTIAN instantly kneels to gather up the mess. JOSHUA also goes for the bread now. CHRISTIAN picks up the pamphlet but doesn't read it thoroughly.

                 "An eyewitness account from Warsaw to Treblinka." You followed the deportations? Good for you!

JOSHUA: Izzy? Bread?

EDEN:	He won't eat. I'll eat his.
JOSHUA:	Izzy?
EDEN:	I missed you, Christian.
CHRISTIAN:	I've missed you. It's becoming harder to get inside the wall.
JOSHUA:	Greetings, Comrade Dabrowski.
IZZY:	Did he bring the guns?
CHRISTIAN:	Liebskind, hello. How is your organization? The... *(Pronounces it laboriously.)* Hashomer Hatzair.
JOSHUA:	Not good. Fifteen deported. Three shot. Comrade Bayla Solomon, Comrade Frederich Blum, Comrade Urik—
IZZY:	Sha, Joshua, eat.
JOSHUA:	He asked.
CHRISTIAN:	So... I bring formal greetings from comrades in the PPS. We heard one hundred thousand were deported.
JOSHUA:	More. Day one, 22,000. Day two, 17,000. Day three—
IZZY:	More, many more.
CHRISTIAN:	You have our sorrow and our rage, as expressed by my presence at this meeting. Wait—who doesn't have his bread?
IZZY:	You eat it. I insist. Did you bring us any guns?
CHRISTIAN:	No! Please eat. Do you know what bread like this means in the Ghetto?

IZZY: No, tell me… Look, the Poles are also starving, or so Eden ceaselessly reminds me in a vain attempt to promote sympathy for the goyim. Take it to your mother. Instead bring me some guns, nu?

CHRISTIAN: Izzy. We eat together as old friends. We don't transact together like businessmen.

IZZY: So, no guns, then—shit.

EDEN: I'll take it. *(She grabs it and bites. To CHRISTIAN.)* It's not about you.

IZZY: Yes, it is. This isn't what we need from him.

JOSHUA: Izzy won't eat bread since the deportations.

CHRISTIAN: But that's crazy.

EDEN: Yes. Joshua says he's worse now than when they took his family.

IZZY: I can hear you!

JOSHUA: He's suffering a delayed reaction.

EDEN: Joshua reads psychoanalysis, like a Viennese bourgeois.

JOSHUA: He has a fascinating case of melancholia of the abject! It's a known neurosis. Because of the deportation bread. They gave away bread for those who came down to the train station. Bread and marmalade.

CHRISTIAN: So, people went willingly?

JOSHUA: They always do. People believe anywhere must be better than here. It defies logic, given their previous experience of Nazi behaviours.

EDEN: Behaviours? Not crimes?

IZZY: It is an international systems-level, multiyear schedule of crimes that began a decade ago: we are all going to be killed by evil people. It's very logical.

CHRISTIAN: That's a conspiracy. I can't accept that logic.

IZZY: Why don't you read that pamphlet again in your hand?

He does. Pause.

See, you might not have to accept reality and carry on believing that people are really good at heart, but we need to know that we're all going to die or no one will fight—Joshy agrees.

CHRISTIAN: But... Poles and Jews will fight together because no one can allow *this* to happen. This will change everything. I can take these pamphlets over to the Aryan side immediately.

EDEN: Yes. Christian will tell them. It's worse than Chelmno. Worse than Wilno.

IZZY: We can't. We only have enough copies for the Ghetto.

EDEN: So, we print more. We can do the printing tonight.

IZZY: All we do is print—I'm going blind.

EDEN: Christian can stay the night and help.

IZZY: I'm sure you would love that, sweetness, but I need to work in the morning.

EDEN: You work in a co-operative barber shop run by Bund comrades.

IZZY: Well, you don't work at all.

EDEN: I would love to go to "work" and debate Trotsky instead of staring at the clock waiting seven hours for a bowl of soup.

IZZY: Don't wait—train—build more bombs.

JOSHUA: This is an example of resolvable creative conflict.

EDEN: I want to go the barber shop too.

IZZY: Fine! Stay. Print as many murder-accounts as you like. And Eden can come to the barber shop. Resolved. *(To CHRISTIAN.)* She just hates being left out of anything.

CHRISTIAN: That's true.

IZZY: She was always at the centre of the circle of girls in the schoolyard in high school.

CHRISTIAN: That's adorable.

EDEN: Stop talking about me.

CHRISTIAN: Have faith, Chaim. And please eat something.

IZZY: Leave me alone with the bread, okay? I'm not suicidal. Let the record reflect that Eden will eat the bread. You're all caught up, Christian? I have neurosis. Everyone was deported. Eden is—

EDEN: Isador!

IZZY: Hungry—she's hungry. I'm not... Let the record show.

JOSHUA: There is no record yet, we haven't called the meeting to order.

IZZY: There's always a record—we're in continuous
                 session: never-ending God-forsaken blighted-
                 with-disease session until we all die too
                 young. That's my current working definition
                 of socialism.

EDEN: Okay—enough time wasting. Start the
                 meeting. We have to look like we get along
                 before the old folks arrive.

                 *The representative attendees of the
                 multilateral meeting bring out the tools
                 they will use to record the meetings and
                 set themselves up. EDEN takes minutes,
                 possibly on the wall. She also takes out a
                 Polaroid camera and photographs the room,
                 and writes the date on the photos and pins
                 it to the wall.*

JOSHUA: I don't think we should call them old folks.

IZZY: When do they get here?

JOSHUA: At three.

EDEN: What time is it now?

IZZY: We sold Joshua's watch, so we don't know.

JOSHUA: For too cheap. I'm upset about it.

EDEN: Christian, what time is it?

CHRISTIAN: *(Sheepishly, because he still owns his watch.)*
                 Twenty after two.

IZZY: Good, so we have forty minutes to end the
                 decades-long disputes between the Bund, the
                 Polish Socialist Party and the Zionists—

JOSHUA: Hashomer Hatzair.

IZZY:

If we don't accomplish this task... Well—there's no if. We have no choice. There were all these fucking ifs six months ago and then Treblinka happened. So, we need to take an oath—today. An oath to fight to the death, with or without the altekakers, but would it be easier with them? Yes. Let's go.

EDEN takes a photo of each person and puts them on the wall, as IZZY does the roll call.

Representing what's left of the Bund we have myself, Comrade Isador Chaim and Comrade Eden Abromavitch. Representing the Zionists, we have Comrade Joshua Liebskind.

JOSHUA:

Hashomer Hatzair. Zionist is not an insult, Izzy.

EDEN:

Don't worry, Joshy, I'm taking minutes. His idiocy won't be recorded.

IZZY:

Fine, the Hashomer Hatzair, who are proud, principled Zionists, even if Zionism is a national colonial project that is doomed to fail, is represented by the reliably humourless Joshua. We also welcome Comrade Christian Dabrowski to the wrong side of the wall who represents the youth flank of the hopefully-still-on-our-side Polish Socialist Party.

CHRISTIAN:

Eden, let the record show that I am here organizing with the Ghetto often, and do not require special welcome.

JOSHUA:

Me too.

EDEN:

So noted. Comrade Chaim is being rude.

IZZY: First item on the agenda will be the passage of the following motion, which I took the liberty of drafting myself: "Whereas we now possess hard evidence that the Nazis plan to deport us all to Treblinka until we are annihilated. Whereas more than half of the Ghetto, some three hundred thousand people were deported to Treblinka this summer. Whereas the complacency with which our people walked like sheep to their deaths makes me sick. Whereas such a fate can be avoided through a united socialist armed resistance and overthrow of the Nazis in Warsaw. Whereas up until now the Jewish Council, known as the Judenrat, has been a useless piece of collaborator shit who refuse to agree with me on this point. Whereas they have finally accepted an invitation to meet and discuss the future of armed resistance against the annihilation of us all. Whereas we need the self-important, and morally ambiguous altekakers of the Jewish leadership to have any hope in hell in organizing a successful military action. Whereas we have a way better chance of getting them to join our coalition if we, the leaders of the youth flanks of the socialist and communist left movements throughout the Ghetto and Warsaw at large, who already agree with this strategy could get over ourselves and form that coalition before they come to this meeting. Whereas I agree that I myself am an ass, and very much part of the reason that our petulant organizations refuse to work together. Whereas Eden has sworn to murder me in my sleep if I don't get over myself. Whereas they will be here in about thirty minutes. Be it resolved that we end the ideological strife and personal breugis that keeps us from becoming one large happy family united in our desire to shoot our way from inside this two-kilometre size mousetrap of certain doom and form a new organizing power whose sole strategic aim is to mount a successful uprising against the Nazis. And we call it the ZOB—the Jewish Fighting Organization. I came up with the name myself.

Okay? All in favour of the motion is everyone. Right?

JOSHUA: Debate.

IZZY: Thirty minutes, Joshua.

JOSHUA: We need to table and debate the motion.

IZZY: Oy vey!

EDEN: No. We pass it, Joshua.

IZZY: ...or do you think I'm being hyperbolic with my use of the phrase "certain doom"? You want to debate certain doom?

JOSHUA: Then what is the point of any of this decorum? Why do we bother to stay civilized and organized at all? Let's just be the animals they think we are!

IZZY: He barely blinks throughout the deportations, but if anyone so much as looks funny at Robert's Rules...

EDEN: Dear God, if I die here at the age of nineteen, I will at least never again have to debate Robert's Rules!

JOSHUA: Make fun of it all you want, but we need—

EDEN: Listen, I understand this gives you nervous feelings, but this is a moment of action, not reflection.

JOSHUA: No—we need to do this properly because of the meeting minutes, Comrade Abromovitch. Our records need to survive us, so they know...

IZZY: *They*...? Who—the goyim? *They* need to know *we* aren't animals, so we need to follow Robert's Rules?

EDEN: Look, don't worry. I've got it here. It's written down. We will send it to the PPS and they will know.

JOSHUA: I move that we open the floor to debate on the motion.

IZZY: Fine. Who cares? Let the record show that we're better than beasts, and that we debated the motion on the eve of our heroic deaths.

CHRISTIAN: Or we can live to tell the tale ourselves?

                Beat.

IZZY: As I was saying...

CHRISTIAN: No! Come on, you doom, and you gloom. We will survive. Say it with me. Eden?

EDEN: I hope we survive.

CHRISTIAN: Say it.

JOSHUA: We might survive.

IZZY: Did he just call us doom and gloom? Am I gloom?

CHRISTIAN: We will fight, and we will live! That's why we fight! To win.

IZZY: The Germans... now they're doom and gloom. When I see them coming towards me in the streets, I think—here comes doom and gloom.

CHRISTIAN: Everyone say: We will survive. Or I'm walking out. I'm sick of this pessimism. I don't find it funny. One, two, three...

ALL BUT IZZY: We will survive.

IZZY: I don't see how, frankly

CHRISTIAN: All of us say it or I'm leaving.

ALL: We will survive.

CHRISTIAN: Okay. I vote in favour of the motion.

IZZY: Really? Great!

CHRISTIAN: We fight to win. Agreed?

IZZY: And you're backed by the PPS?

CHRISTIAN: We've always been with you. The Polish Socialist Party and all we have to offer will fight with the Ghetto.

IZZY: Thank you.

EDEN: Thank God.

CHRISTIAN: You doubted me?

EDEN: Not you, the antisemites among you.

CHRISTIAN: The PPS isn't—

EDEN: No, not the PPS, the other so-called communists.

CHRISTIAN: The AK. Yes, they're nationalist communists.

EDEN: You mean racists.

CHRISTIAN: Officially "Nationalists."

EDEN: You'll explain to me the difference one day, but for now let's just say they don't adore Jews, and the PPS is quickly being devoured by them?

CHRISTIAN: That's not nice. You know it's not true.

EDEN: You remember your brother?

CHRISTIAN: Yes, my brother joined the AK. But that's strategic.

EDEN: Ahhh...

CHRISTIAN: Because we have a better chance united than divided. And he's right. The left has to end all the in-fighting or we haven't got a hope. But I will never join the AK.

EDEN: Because they are antisemites.

CHRISTIAN: Some, admittedly—

EDEN: No, the whole party recently—

IZZY: Eden, stop making problems. The Poles will fight. Good. Let's toast! Eden, get some glasses.

EDEN: Why me getting the glasses?

JOSHUA: We can't yet. I'm afraid Hashomer hasn't given their mandate—

IZZY: No!

JOSHUA: Izzy...

IZZY: No.

JOSHUA: You need to let me speak.

IZZY: No, I don't.

JOSHUA: I'll wait until you're ready to listen.

IZZY: ...because I know what you're about to say—for the record—and it offends me to the depth of my being, Joshua, and I don't want to punch a pacifist.

JOSHUA: I can be patient, Izzy.

IZZY: The goyim will fight with us and you, snivelling babies...

EDEN: Izzy, please. I beg you, let him speak. We have minutes.

IZZY: Shall I tell you what he's going to say? When we die of starvation in the Ghetto or in these gas chambers he hopes it will pressure the British to give us Palestine—is that right? Our deaths will build a case? They want us to die here for their Zionism.

JOSHUA: That's a lie.

IZZY: You're not Zionists before all?

JOSHUA: And I wish you would stop repeating it.

IZZY: You're not Zionists?

JOSHUA: Of course we are, but we don't want Jews to die.

IZZY: What about the Arabs?

JOSHUA: We don't want anyone to die.

IZZY: The Nazis?

JOSHUA: I'm going to ignore you. I apologize if that hurts your feelings. You've made me lose my place. Where was I? Right. I have leave to present the conditions under which we will form a coalition with the Bund and others to create a new organization. What will the organization be called again, Izzy?

IZZY: ZOB. Jewish Fighting Organization. Do you like it?

JOSHUA: You know I don't. But Hashomer Hatzair is a fighting organization, and I'm going to read these out for the record:

CHRISTIAN *helpfully records his list.*

Number one: Will the new coalition, the ZOB... Will we maintain the founding principle of secular, socialist Zionism?

IZZY: No.

JOSHUA: Will you be willing not to be anti-Zionist?

EDEN: Yes. We can do that. Izzy, we can do that.

IZZY: The Bund will never—

EDEN: But the ZOB must.

JOSHUA: Number two: We also ask that we republish the firsthand account of the massacre of Chelmno and the gas trucks at Wilno and deportation to Treblinka and other subsequent evidentiary accounts of the Nazis' extermination agenda to include some of the Hashomer Hatzair's call to relocate Jewish youth to the land of Israel and to organize as socialists there.

IZZY: No.

JOSHUA: We already share the mimeograph, Izzy!

IZZY: Yes, but there are more of us and fewer of you.

JOSHUA: So, might is right?

IZZY: Yes—grow up.

EDEN: Sha, Izzy.

IZZY:`   If I could I would fuck the Zionism out of both of you!

EDEN: Okay—here: I move that we not print anything about where Jews should choose to live until the choice to live somewhere or to live at all is restored to European Jewry. Good?

IZZY: Fine.

JOSHUA: Thank you. Third—

IZZY: Third? I only have two testicles!

JOSHUA: Third: That we fight only when we have a chance to make a difference. When we are armed and when we have enough strength to make a real stand. And that when we do so, we record what we have done and send it to the pilgrims in Palestine to hear our story and to be inspired and fortified by it.

IZZY: It will be a cautionary tale.

JOSHUA: You're wrong, any story of strong Jews is a good story.

CHRISTIAN: For Palestine?

EDEN: For all of us. I agree. Because we are not just Jews, we are socialists—we should print that more often.

> *CHRISTIAN tries to record something that means "Not just Jews, but socialists," feels weird about it crosses out "Just Jews."*

IZZY: Fine, Joshua, you have our permission to
                 write "*the story.*"

JOSHUA: Fourth—

IZZY: No, that's it. You get three.

JOSHUA: Fourth—

EDEN: Joshy, quit while you're ahead.

JOSHUA: I have seven more.

EDEN: Pick one.

JOSHUA: Can we adopt a policy of non-violent
                 communication for our meetings?

IZZY: Nope, and because you chose a stupid one
                 you lost your shot. Okay. Mazal tov. Let's
                 drink.

EDEN: Drink what?

IZZY: Let the record show we drank!

CHRISTIAN: This is extremely exciting. The ZOB! What are
                 we drinking?

IZZY: Potato.

                 *IZZY brings out a corrosive-looking
                 bottle—maybe it's shaped like a gun—
                 from the trap door where they keep their
                 weapons.*

EDEN: That looks vile.

IZZY: It cost me Joshua's watch!

JOSHUA: What?

IZZY: A joke!

EDEN: I'd rather not.

CHRISTIAN:	No, let's drink! Come on, come on, come on. Eden, drink!
EDEN:	Poles are such drunks!
CHRISTIAN:	Jews are so serious!
IZZY:	*(Sings.) The Internationale!*
CHRISTIAN:	Eden drinks! We drink like Poles! I toast! Few people in history have lived so closely together as the Jews and the Poles of Warsaw. May we live bonded in solidarity for generations to come. Cheers.
EDEN:	We are Poles, no? A different religion—so what? To us. The Polish people. Cheers.
IZZY:	What, and the Poles are somehow different from the Russians, or the French? We're Internationals, no?
JOSHUA:	Well, you are—
IZZY:	Long live the International! Cheers!
JOSHUA:	You always cut me off.
	IZZY kisses JOSHUA's cheek.
EDEN:	Why do we need nations at all? We are all just humans. Cheers to humanity!
JOSHUA:	And to the revolution that will let us live like humans.
EDEN:	Yes! All men and women will live and work as equals. With time for joy, and pleasure and fun.
IZZY:	To the communist moshiach that will save mankind!
JOSHUA:	And have you considered the animals?

IZZY:	Too far!
ALL:	Cheers!

They drink their shot. CHRISTIAN writes "communist messiah" in the record.

IZZY:	Good. Now let's talk about how we can kill every last fucking Nazi.
CHRISTIAN:	The Judenrat are coming soon. What's our plan?
EDEN:	We should dominate them.
IZZY:	Good. These Judenrat will pay for their crimes by funding our war chest.
JOSHUA:	We can't ask for charity. We should threaten their lives and then tax them. If we don't have the power to do that, then the Ghetto isn't ready to fight.
IZZY:	You're right. Joshy is right.
JOSHUA:	More than guns right now we need influence.
IZZY:	He's a genius. Drink again. But we also need guns. I'm hoping we can send Christian home with thousands of zloty from this meeting alone.
EDEN:	Is it Czerniakow himself that's coming?
JOSHUA:	We are assured, yes.
EDEN:	That's something—they wouldn't send him if...
IZZY:	If we didn't threaten them! The council could be ours tonight, comrades. So why do I feel like throwing up?

JOSHUA:	Because it took hundreds of thousands of lives to bring them to us?
IZZY:	I think I just hate him a lot. Feh! Can't we just kill him?
EDEN:	Maybe you need to let me do this?
IZZY:	The chairman of the Judenrat won't listen to a girl.
CHRISTIAN:	Sorry to interrupt, but what would you like me to do? I don't want to... you know, take up lots of space. But I was thinking it would be good for me to speak—from the perspective of... what am I? An ally. I could give the conversation some weight, from the perspective of—
EDEN:	I'll let you know when to swoop in and be weighty.
CHRISTIAN:	That's not what I—
IZZY:	Christian, what time is it?
CHRISTIAN:	Ten minutes.
IZZY:	Vomit. What am I supposed to do until then?
JOSHUA:	I suggest that we all rest?
IZZY:	Rest?
EDEN:	Like sleep?
JOSHUA:	Or lie down, at least. Ten minutes of horizontal rest is meant to be intellectually and emotionally restorative according to—
IZZY:	I could have a shlof.
EDEN:	Fine with me.

> *IZZY, EDEN and JOSHUA wander to different corners of the room.*

CHRISTIAN: Yes, you rest—I'll just—

EDEN: Christian, with me.

CHRISTIAN: Yes, I'll just be with Eden.

> *Flimsy curtains are drawn. EDEN and CHRISTIAN begin making out.*

CHRISTIAN: Eden, I want you to know that I...

EDEN: Yes.

CHRISTIAN: I... I think you're...

EDEN: What? Tell me. Do it.

CHRISTIAN: I think you're such a good organizer.

EDEN: What?

CHRISTIAN: I really respect your intellect. Your vocabulary!

EDEN: Gotenyu... Get off me.

CHRISTIAN: What? Why?

EDEN: Off! You think I'm a librarian. Get off.

CHRISTIAN: Okay... Did I say something—?

EDEN: Yes!

CHRISTIAN: Oh. But I really miss you.

EDEN: You miss my vocabulary. Write me a letter.

CHRISTIAN: What is this? You're mad?

EDEN: Why should I be mad?

CHRISTIAN: Oh God... I like your body, too!

EDEN: You like me because I'm an organizer. It's okay, I'm not offended.

CHRISTIAN: But I just told you that I respect you. I honour you. You're not just a...

EDEN: A pretty girl?

CHRISTIAN: Yes! No! You're pretty!

EDEN: Oh, so just shockingly smart for a pretty girl.

CHRISTIAN: I'm confused. My brother told me—

EDEN: Oh, your brother told you to talk about respect?

CHRISTIAN: He has a strong marriage.

EDEN: He's a fascist.

CHRISTIAN: He's traditional.

EDEN: I'm not.

CHRISTIAN: Fine! It's not your mind, it's your breasts! I want your breasts!

EDEN: That's better.

CHRISTIAN: And your face... Your Roman nose.

EDEN: My nose? Yid lover!

CHRISTIAN: What??

EDEN: Isn't that what your brother calls you? *(Laughing at him.)* I'm okay if you have a Jew fetish.

CHRISTIAN: Eden!

EDEN: But only because of your excellent spelling and diction.

CHRISTIAN: Will I have to kiss you to shut you up?

EDEN: Yes please...

                    They continue kissing.

CHRISTIAN: Such a pretty Jewish mouth... Ahhh. Look what you've done to me? *(Referring to his cock.)* We have nowhere to go, do we?

EDEN: In so very many ways.

                    IZZY intrudes.

IZZY: Okay, stop it. We can hear every word.

EDEN: You tell us now?

CHRISTIAN: Sorry, brother.

EDEN: Don't be sorry. They're enjoying it.

IZZY: So are you. I remember how you get.

EDEN: And if I do?

JOSHUA: I'm feeling very embarrassed right now.

IZZY: She's not. She loves it. That's why she's with this boy: To show us how cosmopolitan she is.

EDEN: Tell me what else you know about me.

IZZY: I know that the second this blond beast walked into *our* Bund meeting, you started schlepping for him. But it's not radical, girlchick, and the person I feel bad for is this putz, who is genuinely in love with you.

CHRISTIAN: I'll speak for myself.

IZZY: You'll see when she starts sleeping with a German and dares us all to blink.

CHRISTIAN: Stop! How dare you say that?

EDEN: And if I were with a German? Is he not human? So racist!

IZZY: You would sleep with a Nazi?

EDEN: No! Because they're racists, like you.

IZZY: Well, you do sleep with me. So there.

JOSHUA: I'm observing some creative conflict here.

EDEN/IZZY: Shut up!

CHRISTIAN: May I speak? Eden, he's right that I'm in love with you. I love you even though I'm not Jewish, and I don't care that you are with Izzy sometimes. He thinks this is news to me, but it's not, and I've never cared. You should be with whoever you like. Especially now. Especially here. I love that you want to keep living your life.

EDEN: I wish that's what I feel.

IZZY: The goyim are so… what's the word? Goyish.

EDEN: You are racist.

IZZY: Hopeful.

CHRISTIAN: Jews aren't hopeful?

IZZY: History is happening, and we are history's choice. But I have no hope and neither does she—she whispers as much to me in this room, on that bed…

EDEN: Isador.

IZZY: "We will take as many of them with us as we can before we're killed. Promise me, Izzy…"

                 Beat.

CHRISTIAN: I can't stand this inclination towards darkness. Come on! Let's have faith! Death is common. It's easy. But we're comrades! We're in it together and that's why we'll win the day! Don't snicker. I'm not just saying that. Why shouldn't we?

IZZY: Because you said: win the day—like a putz.

CHRISTIAN: They won't expect us! They won't believe us. If the Ghetto fights in here and the Nazis flank the walls and the PPS and the AK are ready on the outside with all our force we can actually do it. We can take Warsaw back. That's winning the day. Warsaw is one of the greatest civilizations on earth. The entire city will be on our side and we can hold it until the Soviet comrades arrive. It's your plan, Izzy. *You* strategized *this* plan with me weeks ago. To win! Didn't you?

IZZY: Of course I said those things—there are two of me. There are two of every Jew: the one living as hard as they can, righteous and upright. And the other Jew floating above. Recording his despair at this vile world since the day he is born.

EDEN: Very profound…. What the hell have you been reading?

JOSHUA: Kierkegaard. He's been reading *Either Or* since the deportations began.

EDEN: He should stop.

CHRISTIAN: You are too dark for me, Izzy.

IZZY: We are all too dark for you.

EDEN: Don't speak for me. Because you're a Jew and
                 I'm a Jew, so you know me? The way you say
                 goyish like Jews are better than everyone else.

IZZY: I can say the word goyish to my Aryan
                 overlords if I want.

EDEN: They're racist, so you should be too?

JOSHUA: I beg you not to fight over the word "goyish"
                 again. I beg you.

IZZY: I don't dislike goys—but do I think Jewish
                 women should marry them? No. They are
                 trying to kill us—

EDEN: *"They"*… Who's *"they"*?

IZZY: Everyone. And you will have babies with this
                 man if you're lucky enough to survive, and
                 then they won't be Jewish. Fewer Jews. That's
                 all. It's math.

EDEN: Don't count my womb in your math, Isador.
                 Ever.

IZZY: You do Hitler's work for him, that's all.

EDEN: You know who makes women have babies
                 with their own race? Hitler.

JOSHUA: You both have fair points, but you are not
                 having the same conversation.

CHRISTIAN: Joshua, shhh.

JOSHUA: But they're not hearing each other.

EDEN: I hear every word he says.

IZZY: Yes, that's another thing, Joshua. Jews hear every word, and we speak quickly, and we talk over each other, and we make dark jokes. So take this goyish pacifist psychoanalysis book and have some pity on me and throw it out! Please! I beg you!

FELICIA, a well-dressed woman in her fifties, enters the room, tentatively. She pushes the door open with a handkerchief and takes a small step in.

JOSHUA: Actually, it was written by a Jew.

IZZY: Fuck!

FELICIA: Dear God!

IZZY: Who are you?

FELICIA: I'm in the wrong place.

IZZY comes between her and the door.

IZZY: Tell us who you are.

FELICIA: Excuse me? You don't say please? Never mind. I'll go. I'm looking for someone else.

IZZY: Well, you found *us*. Your name, Madam.

FELICIA: Mrs. Felicia Czerniakow.

EDEN: Comrade Chaim, it's the wife.

FELICIA: And who are you? Please.

EDEN: *Oh, if you please, Madam —*

IZZY: Comrade Isador Chaim. Mrs. Czerniakow, we know your husband well.

FELICIA: Oh. So, you are them. Fine…

IZZY: I'm sorry to disappoint.

FELICIA:	That's okay.
JOSHUA:	Will you sit down, Mrs. Czerniakow?
FELICIA:	I don't sit, thank you.
EDEN:	You don't sit.
FELICIA:	No, I prefer not to get lice and so I don't touch walls and I don't sit.
EDEN:	We won't offer to take your coat then.
FELICIA:	Ha! No.
	I will take tea, though. Boiling water kills bacteria. Did you know that, dear?
EDEN:	No tea.
FELICIA:	Ach. It's very hard times. Here. I carry my own. Please, I insist you take it. It's my pleasure, and then we can all have some tea while we talk. It's not as fancy as you might think, in our house, but we have some small privileges and I'm happy to share. Especially with the young people.
EDEN:	Joshua, make us some tea.
FELICIA:	So. Tell me. I didn't hear your names.
EDEN:	I'm Comrade Eden Abromavitch.
JOSHUA:	Comrade Joshua Liebskind.
CHRISTIAN:	Comrade Christian Dabrowski.
FELICIA:	What? My God!
IZZY:	When did you say your husband was arriving?
FELICIA:	But what is he doing here?

EDEN:	Madam looks like she might faint!
FELICIA:	You don't have enough problems?
IZZY:	We can't offer her a chair, though.
FELICIA:	When they catch you they'll kill our people, not yours!
EDEN:	Joshua, stand behind Madam in case she faints.

They laugh.

JOSHUA:	Did you call me? I'm making the tea.
FELICIA:	You're laughing. Fine. Laugh. For some reason it doesn't bother you that he's putting us all in danger. So, maybe I just say what I'm here to say and leave?
IZZY:	I want to speak to the Judenrat.
FELICIA:	I don't know what possessed me to come.
EDEN:	I don't either.
FELICIA:	What a rude young woman you are.
EDEN:	A compliment from Madam!
FELICIA:	You treat everyone like this?
EDEN:	Just capitalist collaborator cows—
IZZY:	Okay, enough—I apologize.
FELICIA:	I'm leaving. Forget I was here. I'm sorry to interrupt all your *"fuck"* and your rudeness.
IZZY:	Where's your husband? He knew Comrade Dabrowski would be here. He's a representative of the Polish Socialist Party.

FELICIA: So, you don't know. I thought you might know already... Oy... It's not easy to say it aloud, just like that... I'm here to inform you that my husband, Senator Adam Czerniakow, has passed away. It happened yesterday. In the most horrible way possible.

She falters.

JOSHUA: Please sit. I beg you. We have no lice.

She sits.

FELICIA: But you don't know that for sure, and you must be vigilant. I try and model vigilance, especially for the young people. Adam is the same. Oh, Adam... I don't even want to say it aloud, but I have to. He killed himself. With poison. He waited until I was out of the house.

EDEN: Oh.

FELICIA: Yes. It's horrible. He was to meet you, today. I know, and I know how important, so I came myself to tell you. Against the advice of the Judenrat, you should know. And I should be at home, in mourning. I have a son. But I came here. Anyway. I'm sure they would have sent someone eventually to tell you, but by then...

EDEN: Dear God...

FELICIA: I know... The Ghetto will mourn once the news gets out. But for now, we're keeping it quiet. It's very hard. Just family, and the Judenrat. Adam was very principled, though, as you know. He kept his word. He kept his appointments. So here I am. Maybe a little tea, my dear.

JOSHUA brings the tea.

It's hard to know what to say in such a moment.

JOSHUA: I'm sorry for your loss, Mrs. Czerniakow.

FELICIA: Thank you. You're the nice one, aren't you?

IZZY: I'm struggling to find words.

FELICIA: He was a great man.

IZZY: No one... No one in the whole Ghetto had the authority that he did.

FELICIA: That's true.

IZZY: He *was* the Judenrat.

FELICIA: Yes. He worked to the bone.

Beat.

IZZY: He had no right.

FELICIA: Excuse me?

IZZY: He had no fucking right!

CHRISTIAN: Izzy!

FELICIA: Are you talking about Adam?

IZZY: Here. Read this.

Gives her the pamphlet.

Did you know? Watch her while she reads. Does she know?

FELICIA: I won't be ordered or shouted—

EDEN: Read it.

She does.

IZZY: Nu?

FELICIA: Do you want me to tell you what it says? I assume you know already. I'm not here to play mind games with you.

EDEN: Mrs. Czerniakow, your husband and the Ghetto police organized the deportations—

FELICIA: Not true. Incorrect.

IZZY: Yes, they did! And now he has an obligation to disband the Jewish council and police and tell the people the truth. He needs to build us our army with the truth! Instead he commits suicide.

JOSHUA: Be easier with her.

EDEN: No! Let him talk. I'm so sick of them, Joshua!

JOSHUA: They don't think like us. It takes them, it takes anyone, time to alter their world view. And the elders are still grieving the world they have lost.

EDEN: So, they're not responsible?

JOSHUA: They are, but it also doesn't matter.

IZZY: Fuck it! If her husband wasn't dead, I would drag him out and shoot him.

CHRISTIAN: Enough, Izzy.

EDEN: No, Christian!

CHRISTIAN: Can I not say—?

EDEN: No, you can't.

CHRISTIAN: It's her husband, not her. Maybe she knew nothing?

FELICIA: No. They're right. I knew everything.

EDEN: What?

FELICIA: They're right. They're rude and disrespectful and savage, but right on all points. There! Did I shock you? Arrogant children...

EDEN: You...

FELICIA: Ha! That shut you up.

EDEN: But you're just his wife...

FELICIA: And your mother is always deferent to her husband? And you're always deferent to whichever of these boys you're fooling around with?

EDEN: We're communists.

FELICIA: No, dear, you're Jewish. Jewish wives don't defer!

EDEN: So you knew what your husband knew.

FELICIA: He told me everything. Every night.

EDEN: How do you sleep?

FELICIA: We don't! You think we sleep? Do you know what it's like to do these... these bone-crushing calculations of who lives and who dies? But someone had to do it and we were those people. And we were a little bit hopeful that every day would bring us closer to the end of the war.

IZZY: Hope is poison.

FELICIA: Maybe. But we did what we thought was right together. Until yesterday. Yesterday is what happens when a husband acts on his own, without consulting a wife. And I agree! He had no right! He left me. In this hell.

IZZY: You knew he was coming to see us?

FELICIA: It was me who told him he must! But he was stalling. Oy God... He was doing it for me. That's what no one knew, until now. Here, now you read.

             IZZY takes the letter she is offering.

             Yes, you. The rude young man in charge.

IZZY: I'm not in charge.

FELICIA: Whatever you say.

IZZY: A suicide note.

FELICIA: Yes. Read it. *(He does.)* And now you see?

IZZY: It says that yesterday he tried to negotiate with the SS that Korczak's orphans be spared deportation. ....And that he failed. He's racked with guilt and he begs your forgiveness.

EDEN: They're deporting the orphanage!

FELICIA: It's done. This will happen in the morning.

EDEN: We can do something!

FELICIA: No, you can't. Just keep reading.

IZZY: It says they threatened to deport you, Felicia. That for the past many weeks, they threatened your life if he didn't comply.

FELICIA: Right. So, it's me. My fault.

IZZY: You're only one woman.

FELICIA: I agree! But he didn't ask me. He made his choice. Which of you could say that you wouldn't do the same?

EDEN: I wouldn't.

FELICIA: Ha. And you know what? I believe you. But this one here, this Mr. Christian? He would for you, I'll bet.

EDEN: You don't know anything about us.

FELICIA: Of course, I do. You think you invented the wheel? Okay—so it was selfish of him to spare me. But you can at least admit that you understand? And now that he's dead, some of it will stop for a brief moment. They can't manage without Adam's... help.

EDEN: Help!

FELICIA: And he killed himself so they would stop. At least for a few days. Hopefully a few weeks. Adam's death gives us some time.

IZZY: Us?

FELICIA: Yes, you heard me. The Judenrat is in shambles. They all have wives too. They will certainly let you flounder here. Either way. if you want to step over the Judenrat, it's now or never.

IZZY: She's right. Now is the time to act.

FELICIA: I want to help you. That much I can do. So? Shall we call this meeting to order?

Someone goes to write on the minutes. Someone else snaps a picture of the room and writes the date and pins it to the wall.

Intermission.

"Forever Young" by Rod Stewart may be used as intermission music.

Rich Jews/Poor Jews

Not all Jews are rich. Not all Jews are rich. Today or ever. Swelling below the relatively few affluent Jews in Poland was a massive Jewish Proletariat. Hundreds of thousands of working-class people. They were largely urbanites, unionists and on some spectrum of the communist left. The Holocaust annihilated a whole civilization: Yiddish Socialist Europe.

Class War in the Ghetto

Having money helped some Jews survive the Holocaust. Having money helps anyone survive anything. When the Nazis invaded Poland and began their assault on Jews, class divisions widened. The Jewish Councils, the Judenrat, fed the Germans' demand for slave labour with lower-class Jews.

The characters in this play are not just from mildly different backgrounds or generations. They were at war. People like Felicia Czerniakow would have been complicit, if not directly responsible for killing socialists because they were socialists.

Towards the end of 1942 everything changed very quickly. Nazis liquidated rich and poor alike, and the plan to exterminate all Jews, not just problematic ones, was becoming obvious. Class division had expanded because of the war, but then rapidly contracted. Only under life-or-death circumstances was the ruling class willing to collaborate with the working class to protect themselves.

The Rise of the ZOB

By winter 1943, the ZOB were quickly gaining authority and military power inside the Ghetto and there were a few hundred trained ZOB fighters, not four.

They didn't forget the betrayals of the upper class. They were taxing their wealth, or *expropriating*, to use the correct Marxist terminology. The money was being put towards the good of the whole. They were spending it on weapons.

These tactics of waging urban guerrilla warfare did not begin or end here. They were passed to revolutionaries to come in Latin America, for example, who then taught them directly to the Black Panthers and the Weather Underground in the U.S. A good question is: Who is learning these lessons now?

The instruction under the ZOB was to resist, which meant death. It was not an instruction to survive, but rather to choose your own death. Remarkably, the people were listening, and when they defied Nazi orders and were killed for it, they were heralded as heroes. But meanwhile, these heroes who supplanted the police and the government simply by publishing pamphlets... I mean, they were still just teenagers, trapped in a room.

The Story of Solidarity

> *Everything is the same, only it looks as though the young people are now living permanently in the room. IZZY is lying on the cot in the room. He's weak and he has spastic coughing. There is a tattered folding screen set up around his cot. FELICIA is on the opposite corner of the room, copying out some text.*

IZZY: *(Shouts out of nowhere.)* How can death be so boring?

FELICIA: I'll check your temperature.

> *FELICIA puts a scarf over her mouth, walks lightly to IZZY, checks his temperature and covers him with a blanket. He allows her. Hands her a page he's writing. She goes back to her desk. JOSHUA enters, with a bowl of "soup."*

FELICIA: His fever is gone, Baruch Hashem.

JOSHUA: Izzy? Here. *(Gives him soup.)*

IZZY: I said no, sweetness.

JOSHUA: Please. Please? You need to eat.

IZZY: You need to eat.

JOSHUA: I ate! I got an extra bowl and a bit of bread. And there was a potato in my soup, and I ate it.

IZZY: You're very cute when you lie.

JOSHUA: Uch, I know!

IZZY: You know how cute you are?

JOSHUA:	You keep calling me cute, so it stands that I'm cute. We're digressing from the soup.
IZZY:	Handsome too. Such cheekbones.
JOSHUA:	You cause me a lot of stress.
IZZY:	So I can see your sweet cheeks blush.
JOSHUA:	But the soup, Izzy!
FELICIA:	Isador, eat the soup right now, please.

IZZY eats the soup. EDEN enters with a giant milk canister.

EDEN:	Izzy, you look worse.
IZZY:	I'm a wilted flower. I'm Kierkegaard.
EDEN:	Mrs. Czerniakow, did you see what I got? Look, it's perfect!
FELICIA:	Good work, Medele!
EDEN:	I used your name and spoke to the wife!
FELICIA:	She owes me, big! He thinks he's a big macher, but the wife is my creature.
IZZY:	Did we get milk?
EDEN:	No, it's empty. It's for burying the minutes. We talked about this.
IZZY:	We're burying the minutes?
EDEN:	You were in the meeting. You just tune out when we talk about anything other than shooting. And we should consider burying other things too. Letters from our fallen comrades. Maybe art? Schulich's play?
IZZY:	Where are we burying the milk?

FELICIA: So, I've taken the liberty of drafting a little map. *(She pins the map on the record.)* Look. The Ghetto divides into the old and new sections, as you know—and if I understand we have divided the fighting cells into four blocks, correct? So, why don't we bury them each under the care of the fighting organizations to ensure at least one survives the fight, and I know exactly the right spots!

JOSHUA: Eden and Izzy, can I speak to you a second?

FELICIA: No one knows this city like I do! Hehehe!

JOSHUA: Now, please! I'm insisting. Insisting!

EDEN: He insists...

> They huddle around IZZY's cot to speak in "private."

JOSHUA: Eden, did you give Mrs. Czerniakow the maps of our quadrants and battle plans?

EDEN: Um... Yes... She asked!

JOSHUA: It was entrusted to you, not the Judenrat. *(To IZZY.)* I don't know if I can organize with her in the room like this.

EDEN: Who, me?

JOSHUA: No. Czerniakow.

IZZY: Why? She comes every day for months, and you want me to tell her to stop?

IZZY: Let her come. She brings tea.

EDEN: She's very sincere. Look at her...

JOSHUA: I don't dispute that—

EDEN: So, what?

JOSHUA:	*Socialism.* We don't organize with capitalists.
IZZY:	Don't be stupid. We have to organize the capitalists. We have to recruit the rats to fight.
JOSHUA:	Hashomer has principles. Socialism, being the most central—
EDEN:	It's a word.
JOSHUA:	It's the word that brings us together, Eden.
IZZY:	No, that word is "Jew."
JOSHUA:	Disagree. Socialism brings us weapons from the PPS. It brings us someone like Christian from under the wall. We fight for the revolution. Our one uniting principle: Does it empower the workers? Does it make more socialists? She wants to go back to her six-thousand-zloty house, that's what brings her here.
IZZY:	Shh... You're hurting my head. We are fighting to kill Nazis and that's the end of the story.
JOSHUA:	It can't be. That can't be—
IZZY:	That's the end of *our* story. For us, this is the end.
JOSHUA:	I don't accept—
IZZY:	I get it, my sweet. You feel alive when you hold your principles. So hold them.
JOSHUA:	I'm not being emotional. I'm trying to reconcile—
IZZY:	It's better you shouldn't. Just keep working. Even Mrs. Czerniakow isn't dumb enough to believe she's going back to her house on the hill.

EDEN sits on the bed with IZZY.

EDEN: Oy, I feel sick.

IZZY: You feel sick a lot these days...

EDEN: Relax, it's probably just a bit of TB, like you.

IZZY: Pardon me, I have rickets!

EDEN: And TB. Don't worry, I won't stop lying with you ...because it's the only bed.

IZZY: Joshy, you can come too. There's room.

FELICIA: Scarfs! Children, I beg you—scarfs!

             They all reluctantly put scarfs on their mouths.

             Your noses too!

             They pull up their scarfs.

             Good.

IZZY: Anyway, this reminds me of a good midrash. Do you know the one about the Jews at the Red Sea?

EDEN: Really? You're doing Torah study?

IZZY: Yes! Cuddle close, Kinderlach. I don't have TB. It was Rebbi Bolton who told me this one. You remember him from shul? He had some sponge cake and a little glass of brandy and I was saying something contrary and idiotic trying to get attention at the expense of being punished and the Rebbi said, "Yeshaayahu, listen, the Jews are a paradox. You know why? Because when we were Israelites, before we had the Torah from Moshe Rabenu, we went into the sea. We walked into the Red Sea because the Egyptians were chasing us and we had no choice, so we walked into an ocean to die instead of turning around and going back into bondage. And that's what happened. We died there. But also, we did not die! We lived. We came out the other side by God's grace, became legendary. It doesn't make sense, but both things are true. We died there, but we also lived." That's what we are doing here, in my bed where I do and do not have tuberculosis.

JOSHUA: I don't get it.

IZZY: You're killing me, Joshy!

JOSHUA: I'm not good with metaphors.

IZZY: Dying and living at the same time!

JOSHUA: That's impossible.

IZZY: I don't have the strength to explain paradox to you, right now.

JOSHUA: I understand the definition. I just don't like it.

FELICIA: (*From across the room.*) Okay! I'm done! I transcribed the whole pamphlet. It forbids any Jew from willingly walking out to be deported for any reason, on pain of treason and summary execution under the authority of the ZOB. I think it's quite strong.

               FELICIA brings a transcribed pamphlet over to IZZY's bedside to show the group.

IZZY: That's so much better.

FELICIA: You see? Penmanship! I have excellent handwriting. There were thirteen spelling errors, by the way. And you kept changing tense between the past and the present. Which one did you want?

IZZY: The present/

JOSHUA: The past.

FELICIA: Never mind. I chose the present tense, and I'm not copying it out again. But it's not badly written. Much better than your last one. I'm going to give this one to my nephew and he'll pass it to his friends.

EDEN: Your nephew who sits on the Judenrat now?

FELICIA: So? He's a good boy.

EDEN: Boy? Isn't he old? Like thirty?

FELICIA: He's very "left-wing." Sympathetic from the inside. He's a comrade almost!

JOSHUA: *(Mouths to IZZY.)* "Comrades"?

IZZY: Comrade Czerniakow, come join us.

JOSHUA: We should work.

IZZY: No, we should play. Oh, good idea. Let's play a game!

JOSHUA: We must get these printed and I need to find some food for tonight for my family—

EDEN: Yes, a game! If I don't distract myself, I'm going to eat the feathers from this pillow and pretend it's chicken. Let's play: Where would we be right now if…?

JOSHUA: That sounds like the worst game in the world.

IZZY: I get it. I like it. This is it: If we were not Jews, where would we be right now?

EDEN: No! You're obsessed with Jews. If we were not in a war, where would we be right now? Felicia, you go. Where would you be if not here?

FELICIA: You want me to play? That's nice. Okay. But you can be Jews and be in the war and still not be here.

EDEN: What do you mean?

FELICIA: You're here because you're fighters. If you were not such troublemakers, where would you be right now?

IZZY: No. How about just this: In real, normal life where would we be right now? Eden!

FELICIA: Married! She'd be married.

EDEN: No!

IZZY: Yes! But to who?

EDEN: Never!

IZZY: Liar.

EDEN: I would be in school, I hope. Or just working in the factory next to Mama, if I'm unlucky.

IZZY: Such a self-hating proletarian! You can do better work from that factory than you can from a university.

EDEN: Says the rich kid.

JOSHUA: I could hardly afford high school.

IZZY: So, Joshua would be working.

JOSHUA: Maybe for the syndicalist union. I want to keep the books for them. I'd be good at that, right, Izzy?

IZZY: Absolutely.

JOSHUA: And I would be preparing to go to Palestine.

EDEN: Ugh, why? I never want to leave Warsaw. Did you know my parents were Russian farmers?

IZZY: You think I never noticed that you're a peasant?

EDEN: Shut up. They came here to escape antisemitism. That's the joke.

IZZY: Well, I'd be in medical school. I would be writing a Friday morning exam.

EDEN: You think you would have gotten in?

IZZY: What? How dare you! I'm very smart and wealthy.

EDEN: You're smart, wealthy *and* distracted. You would just go from café to bar to the Bund and you'd forget about the deadline for the entrance exam or something—but then you'd argue with the dean to try and let you do it again. And he would! But then you'd forget to show up again.

IZZY: You'd remind me, girlchick. You'd come to my house and wake me up on the morning of the exam. Do you think we would still be together, you and me? And we would have found Joshua too, of course. The child sitting in the back of the meeting, looking very serious.

JOSHUA: I'm only two years younger than you!

FELICIA: Sha… You're all children.

EDEN: Probably we'd be together.

IZZY: Okay, that's where I'll be. Wherever you guys are.

EDEN: Christian would be with us too, though.

IZZY: Never mind… I'd be going out for a cigarette.

JOSHUA: You would smoke?

FELICIA: So, you want to hear me? I know exactly where I would be. The butcher. It's Shabbos.

             IZZY laughs.

             You laugh, but if you don't get there first thing, it's a bloodbath with actual blood. You should see it when there's one chicken and four women.

IZZY: I know, I'm laughing because my mother would be there with you.

FELICIA: Who's your mother? Do I know her?

IZZY: Maybe, but she's probably dead.

FELICIA: So, she doesn't have a name?

IZZY: Agnes Chaim.

FELICIA: I don't know her. But I think she's still alive, Isador. You'll see. So, me and Agnes—first we would buy the chicken and then we would take it over to the schoychet and no matter what we would always get blood on our shoes, and then over to the feathers lady— because who wants to do their own feathers, right?

JOSHUA: I used to do the feathers in my house. My mother and sisters sew all day Friday. I would go get the chicken, do the feathers, take care of the kids until they were done and then I would go out to a Hashomer meeting.

FELICIA: On Shabbos?

JOSHUA: Always.

FELICIA:	Why do it on Shabbos? Just to upset your parents?
JOSHUA:	It's a youth movement.
FELICIA:	So? You have to be sacrilegious youth?
JOSHUA:	Secular. Mrs. Czerniakow, do you wonder if maybe you don't belong here with us, since you don't agree with our principles?
IZZY:	Joshua, sha. Go back to the chicken soup.
FELICIA:	I belong here because these *youth* of yours need lots of help. God wants me here, I think.
JOSHUA:	We don't believe in God.
FELICIA:	He says as if I care. So, listen, I have a good idea. We should kill a few Jews.
JOSHUA:	Oh my God! You see?
FELICIA:	Bad Jews! Traitors!
JOSHUA:	Such as Adam Czerniakow?
FELICIA:	No, smart pants, I mean the Jewish Police. These monsters, who for a loaf or two of bread will do horrible things, tearing a child away from his parents on the street to march him to the wall to be the audience watching when another child is executed for smuggling.
JOSHUA:	The Judenrat is the Jewish Police. They are the same.
FELICIA:	That's not true! Adam and I spent every night figuring out how to save more people. And then all day, every day Adam pleaded with them. Begged them for ten lives, a hundred lives... ten more days, a thousand more potatoes... Whatever he could get. Just

because he failed doesn't mean he wasn't trying. The Jewish Police are thugs, trained by these Ukrainians, who are also thugs with their Jew-hating souls.

EDEN: Forgive me for missing the nuance.

FELICIA: It matters. What you are trying or not trying to do matters. What are you all doing here, if trying doesn't matter? You don't know you will win. You probably won't. Is that so different from my Adam? Tell me something, Eden, did you watch the deportations?

EDEN: How could I? I was hiding.

FELICIA: I watched. I made myself watch. I could have stayed inside. It was the Blue Police and the Ukrainians swarming the ghetto like wasps. These *Jews* working so efficiently with the SS on the outside. They divided up the roles, called everyone down, and they shot whoever was left upstairs. Block by block. And the people stood there, some holding nothing, some holding everything, but all of them knew they were caught and that was their faces: it was the end of their hope. And then the Umschlag. Oy, the Umschlag... You don't know.

EDEN: The train platforms? You didn't see that. How could you?

FELICIA: No, but I heard. Firsthand. A few got away and came back to tell the Judenrat, as if Adam could do a single thing about it. I'll tell you, there are people waiting there for days. The transports can only take twelve hundred every time, and they've marched tens of thousands there. Can you imagine, they're begging and bribing to be put on a train to be sent to Treblinka. But the families wait in starvation, with thirst in a couple of school buildings, where the floors have turned to toilets and mothers are clutching their children. They have nothing left to do but perish.

EDEN: They could fight back. You say there are tens of thousands.

FELICIA: How? No one has organized anything. To fight is just to kill yourself. They're holding their children.

EDEN: That's a single thing your Adam could have done. He could have organized or allowed us to organize.

FELICIA: She thinks she tells me something I don't know already. Why do you think I'm here? I like being organized. I believe in organizing things. I taught my kids to be organized. I can help you.

EDEN: You mean we can help you.

FELICIA: I can keep you kids clean, and I can care for Izzy, and I can keep typing and editing. Let me.

IZZY: Let her.

JOSHUA: We never took a vote. This isn't minuted anywhere.

IZZY: Joshua...

JOSHUA: Mrs. Czerniakow is not in our minutes. No one knows she is here, do they, Izzy?

IZZY: Look, Liebskind, I know it calms you to minute things.

JOSHUA: I'm calling us to order.

                 He jumps up and starts taking minutes.

                 I think we need to preserve her presence for
                 the record if she is here.

IZZY: We can't. Are you crazy? Our people will kill
                 us, and her people will kill her.

JOSHUA: Which is exactly why I would like to speak
                 against any motion for her to organize with
                 us, in accordance with our bylaws.

IZZY: Gevalt...

JOSHUA: She's not one of us, Izzy. She's always safe.
                 She's always been safe.

EDEN: For the record, I understand what he's saying.
                 How many times have the police beaten her
                 in the streets? How many times has she sent
                 police to beat us in the streets?

                 JOSHUA records "Beats us in the streets."

FELICIA: Never.

EDEN: Before the war, even?

JOSHUA: Thank you, Comrade. I move to state for
                 the record that we are at war with Felicia
                 Czerniakow. Class war and she is not a
                 comrade.

IZZY: She is turning into a communist before our
                 very eyes.

FELICIA: I'm not a communist.

JOSHUA: Of course not!

FELICIA: But do communists have a monopoly on
                 doing the right thing? What does it have to
                 do with communism?

JOSHUA: Everything.

FELICIA: The Jewish Police are damned by God, not communists.

JOSHUA: I will explain: Fighting Nazis without class struggle is like helping the Jewish proletariat survive now, so you can kill us later.

FELICIA: Either I'm a communist or I'm a killer?

JOSHUA: Yes, that's right. What's more, your bourgeoisie will be the Jews who survive this war because you have money, and then *you* will tell *our* story. You will shake your head and say: if only they were more lucky or *smart*, they might have survived. You will pity our poverty without ever remembering how strong our workers' solidarity drives us to be. Her presence here is absurd.

FELICIA: You're very lucky no one has ever given you any power, young man. With great power comes great responsibility.

JOSHUA: Power is corruption and violence. But it's true everyone has some power. We are all oppressors in some ways. Even us socialist Jews.

IZZY: Who do I oppress? The cockroaches?

JOSHUA: Or how about me? Have you ever thought about how you have power over—

IZZY: Let's not burden our friends with our bedroom spats.

JOSHUA: Have you considered the ethics of interrupting me when I talk?

EDEN: Yeah, have you, Izzy?

IZZY: I'm just trying to make everyone laugh, a
            little!

EDEN: You need to grow up.

IZZY: No! I'm young. We're young! How old do
            you want me to get? How fast do you need
            me to get old? Can't I just flirt and tease and
            be me? I'm starving—

EDEN: Who isn't?

IZZY: …Emotionally. Sexually. Intellectually. I'm
            lying here—I can barely stand. My body is
            like an old ugly man! Just let me be me.

JOSHUA: No.

IZZY: Really?

JOSHUA: The world outside still exists. Her wealth and
            her sins still exist. This is the game we are
            playing, right? Not where would we be, but
            who are we outside this room?

IZZY: So we have to be serious and joyless?

JOSHUA: No, but we have to think hard about how to
            live because—

IZZY: Because we don't have much time left?

JOSHUA: Always.

IZZY: Every boring, pain-filled minute. That
            sounds really bad.

JOSHUA: I need to think.

IZZY: I don't. I need to do.

            *IZZY pulls himself up and hobbles over to
            where the minutes are and writes "Killing
            some Jews."*

So, Felicia, that's a good idea! Shooting some Jewish Police has been high on our list for a while. We tried to assassinate Captain Szerynski. You may have heard.

He goes to his cache of weapons and pulls up the trap door, with some effort.

FELICIA: We heard.

IZZY: Botched it.

FELICIA: You scared him.

IZZY: Really?

FELICIA: He was screaming at Adam, all red and flailing.

IZZY: That's so nice of you to say. But back then we had only a few bullets. Now we have more. Did I show you the arsenal?

He pulls out a few guns and bullets and fondles them.

FELICIA: You mean the cellar?

IZZY: It's a trap door for ghosts and murder!

FELICIA: You showed me your guns. Very impressive. Good for you.

IZZY: My point is not to admire my guns, but that you should understand the meaning of my guns. They mean that we can afford to kill some Nazis now. Eden, what do you think? There are those hideous two monsters who sit by the wall to shoot at children smugglers. Let's shoot back.

EDEN: Yes. Kill the Blue Police and the Nazis. Both.

JOSHUA: So we're at the killing part now?

IZZY: We were already there, Joshua.

JOSHUA: One failed assassination isn't the same as—

IZZY: Sweetness here was hoping we would all be deported before we got to the killing part.

JOSHUA: Please don't insult me. I dread violence.

EDEN: How are you a member of Hashomer?

JOSHUA: I love Hashomer. I would die for it. But can I kill?

IZZY: You can. You're going to kvetch at us first, but Joshy is going to kill our first Nazi.

FELICIA: No, Jew! Let's get Jakob Lejkin, their lieutenant. He's a rotten pestilent schmuck.

IZZY: I really think we need to kill a German. Publicly. We need to show the Ghetto that they can die like any human, and more than that, that Jews can kill them.

JOSHUA: That sounds very poetic, but it will bring the full retribution of the Reich down on the Ghetto. Is that what you want?

IZZY: Yes.

EDEN: Yes, but not now. Not until we're ready, Izzy.

IZZY: Not you too! Go sit over there with Joshy. Felicia and I are in war council.

EDEN: We're not ready.

IZZY: Yes! We are! Every fighting man and woman in the ZOB. is ready. For weeks! We are trained. We are waiting. We have more power than any other Ghetto institutions. But we can't fight? We wait—fuck, I can't stand up.

FELICIA: Lie down.

EDEN: We're waiting for—

IZZY: For Christian with the guns we bought three weeks ago!

EDEN: You speak like he's me. I'm not responsible for my boyfriend.

IZZY: Ah ha! You admit that he's your boyfriend!

EDEN: Good God. Do you think we communicate psychically? I wish I knew where he was. He could have been caught in a tunnel weeks ago. It's horrifying.

IZZY: Because you love him!

EDEN: Because I want the guns!

JOSHUA: Izzy is just jealous.

IZZY: Yes, I'm just jealous.

EDEN: I really hate it when you treat me like a woman!

FELICIA: What a strange thing to say... Your generation is strange.

EDEN: I agree we should kill the Jewish police captain first.

                EDEN goes to the map FELICIA drew and elaborates on it.

                Then, when Christian arrives with more weapons, we tell him to ready the PPS for the ambush. It won't take many bullets to make them run.

JOSHUA: Run?

EDEN: Because they won't want to die like this. They won't want to be killed by Jews.

IZZY: So, they'll run away…

EDEN: They won't understand that we can fight. But the PPS and all of Warsaw will know because of the assassinations that we are ready, and they'll be ready on the outside too. Our PPS and AK comrades will kill the fleeing Germans for us.

IZZY: How beautiful will that be?

EDEN: We could win.

IZZY: If Christian comes, maybe we can win.

EDEN: For a few days, if the whole ghetto fights, we can win. I'm certain that maybe we can win. Joshua, remember you said that you will fight when we can win?

JOSHUA: I remember.

EDEN: Felicia?

FELICIA: Me? Sure! Why not think we can win? L'chaim! So, Eden, where's—

EDEN: I don't know where he is!

FELICIA: …the ink for the mimeograph because I have to get home soon to say Kaddish for Adam.

EDEN: Oh. Sure. How quaint.

FELICIA: Not the word I would use for our ancient prayer of mourning, but whatever you say.

EDEN: I'm sorry. None of us are religious.

JOSHUA: That's not true. Izzy is.

EDEN: No, he's not.

JOSHUA: He told me he believes in God.

EDEN: *What?* Since when?

JOSHUA: Fourteen months ago.

EDEN: Communists are not religious.

JOSHUA: I wonder if you feel jealousy because you see that Izzy and I have a friendship that doesn't involve you.

FELICIA: Oy, God. Just ask him. Izzy? Do you believe in God?

IZZY: I'm sleeping...

FELICIA: Do you believe in God?

IZZY: That fucker? Yes, of course.

FELICIA: Don't swear about God like that!

EDEN: Seriously?

IZZY: Sure. I'm Orthodox now. When there's less lice, I'm growing a beard and marrying a nice Jewish girl.

FELICIA: I have a niece who went Orthodox.

IZZY: She sounds perfect. Now let me sleep.

EDEN: I can't tell if he's serious. Are you being serious?

IZZY: Completely. Joshua will go to Palestine. I'm going Orthodox. Eden, you're going to go full goy, I imagine.

EDEN: No. But I don't think that my father lives in the sky with a long white beard and commands me to make babies because that is dumb.

FELICIA: You know what I think? You took God and switched him with Marx. They both have white beards and lots to say.

EDEN: You read Marx?

FELICIA: I was nineteen once.

EDEN: Just how old are you?

FELICIA: How old do you think I am?

EDEN: Old. Like forty-five.

FELICIA: You could be a bit more respectful of age.

EDEN: You could be a bit more respectful of Marx.

IZZY: And I think we should read more Kierkegaard. That man was funny. I need to sleep now. No more blah blah blah.

CHRISTIAN sends a signal of lights and footsteps to the stage. He enters carrying a wooden crate and another milk canister.

IZZY: THANK GOD! Baruch Ha-fucking-shem! Christian, get in here you glorious, sexy Polack! I would kiss you, but I have TB. Show me, show me, show me!

CHRISTIAN: Ten potatoes! Bread! Some beef!

FELICIA: What did you do? This is a feast! Joshua, take this for your family. And...?

CHRISTIAN: ...and... look underneath!

IZZY: Bring me the box!

CHRISTIAN: Yes, you do the honours, Comrade Chaim.

IZZY: Hey, hey! Grenades! Kerosene! Guns! Bullets! Eden, kiss him!

EDEN:	I will!

They do.

JOSHUA:	Comrade, it is wonderful to see you.
CHRISTIAN:	My friends, I am so sorry for my long absence. I am so sorry, Eden.
EDEN:	Is that fucking cheese?
CHRISTIAN:	Yes. Please eat it. How are you? Eden, you look beautiful. Liebskind, you look good. Chaim... Can you walk?
IZZY:	Of course, of course. I'll have some of this food Eden is inhaling.
EDEN:	It's so so good... You have an appetite, Izzy?
IZZY:	I'm fine. I'm better than fine. Look at my new stuff! Christian, help me open the ghost trap!
FELICIA:	Are you certain no one saw you come here, Mr. Dabrowski?
CHRISTIAN:	You're still here, I see, Mrs. Czerniakow.
IZZY:	She's our new friend.
CHRISTIAN:	She is?
FELICIA:	The Blue Police, may their names be a curse upon their children's heads, want me dead— but so what? I don't care. I'm a truth-teller now!
IZZY:	She's a truth-teller now! What else did you miss? Same old doom and gloom. Edelstein and Bartok were caught smuggling our newspapers and they hung twenty Jews alongside them.
CHRISTIAN:	May they rest in peace.

FELICIA: May their memories be for a blessing.

IZZY: We have to fight soon, Christian. There will be a window between now and another liquidation.

CHRISTIAN: Yes. We must. We will.

IZZY: That's what I want to hear.

CHRISTIAN: Let's eat first. We can talk later.

EDEN: Izzy, you take the cheese. I think it's actually making me a bit sick...

FELICIA: Okay—I'll leave you young people to your meal. I'm glad to see you back, Comrade Dabrowski.

CHRISTIAN: Comrade!

FELICIA: Why not? It's fun to be part of a gang!

              FELICIA leaves.

CHRISTIAN: Tell me more about what I've missed.

JOSHUA: Izzy is sick.

CHRISTIAN: But that doesn't stop him!

IZZY: That doesn't stop me! What other fun news? Oh, we're going to kill a Jewish Police commander. An evil man by the name of Jakob Lejkin.

CHRISTIAN: Good. How can I help with that?

IZZY: We don't need your help with that.

CHRISTIAN: I want to be helpful.

EDEN: We know.

IZZY: Joshua has been ordered to do it.

JOSHUA: I have?

IZZY: Didn't you hear me say?

JOSHUA: You said I would kill our first Nazi. This murder—

IZZY: Assassination.

JOSHUA: Does he have a family?

IZZY: Why?

JOSHUA: Because I need to know things.

CHRISTIAN: Joshua, did I ever tell you about my uncle who was a farmer?

JOSHUA: No.

CHRISTIAN: He's a farmer about a day's walk outside the city. Dairy. And he loves his cows. He's an old bachelor, in spite of my mother's disdain for it, and he's been working the dairy since he was a teenager and, well, the cows are his best friends. Don't laugh! It's true. The man loves his cows like friends and children. And then this cursed war came, and the Germans stole half of his cattle. He wept. Then they give us these rations that will make us starve to death. Like you, only slower.

IZZY: Slower would be better.

CHRISTIAN: And farmers are only allocated a small amount of feed for their livestock. What's he to do? Our whole family is hungry. So he decides that instead of trying to get his hungry, dried-out cows to milk, he will slaughter them and feed as many people as he can. He will keep a few goats for milk, you can thank him for that cheese you're eating. He wrote me a letter about this.

EDEN: I remember. He showed me this letter.

CHRISTIAN: It says that he thinks of me as the moral centre
               of our family. That I'm his favourite nephew,
               and so he's chosen to tell me of his decision
               to kill his cows for meat. I wrote back right
               away. I told him that I would come to the farm
               straightaway and that I would do it to spare
               him from having to slaughter his friends.
               When I got there, though, the task had been
               done. I asked him, Uncle, didn't you get my
               letter? He said he did, but he could never
               have let anyone else do it. He slaughtered
               every one of them and mourned each cow,
               even though he was the one to kill them.

EDEN: That's beautiful.

CHRISTIAN: That's Joshua. He does what's correct. He'll
               kill when it's right and he'll mourn too. Let's
               all give him a break.

JOSHUA: It's not up to me to murder people. At some
               point in some moment we need to stop
               harming one another. But that moment is not
               now.

CHRISTIAN: Exactly.

JOSHUA: Because we are at this part of the war, not
               another.

CHRISTIAN: I, too, hold hope for forgiveness later on, at
               the end.

JOSHUA: The problem… *My* problem is that I can't
               imagine the end anymore. It's just the Ghetto.
               Sometimes it's just this room. I agree, that if
               the world is this Ghetto, then we will have to
               commit murder.

CHRISTIAN: Joshua can be counted on.

IZZY: *(JOSHUA gets a kiss from IZZY.)* Okay—let's toast. Come here, guys. Come here, come here... I really love you all so much. Get the potato, Eden.

EDEN: Okay, why not?

JOSHUA: You want to toast to my willingness to kill?

IZZY: I want to toast to you. Look what you've done to me... Eden, pour it out to the last drop. Help me up. If it was not for you all, my comrades, my lovers... So here is to the past and to the future and most of all to the ZOB!

IZZY / JOSHUA /
EDEN: To the ZOB.

EDEN: Christian, drink!

CHRISTIAN: I need to tell you something first.

EDEN: Okay. Good news, I hope.

CHRISTIAN: Some good. I've secured more supplies. Gasoline for explosives. And I will buy you twelve more boxes of bullets by next week. The PPS will buy them for you.

IZZY: To our brothers and sisters in the Polish Socialist Party! Drink!

CHRISTIAN: Just wait. There are seven pistols still coming along with the ones I have brought you here. And a few rifles. This is from the PPS. We are with you.

IZZY: I never doubted.

EDEN: Yes, you did. He definitely did.

IZZY: Only once or twice a day. Now drink!

CHRISTIAN: Wait. Please. A motion was passed last night. The PPS and the AK need to delay their... military unit contributions.

IZZY: What?

CHRISTIAN: Their physical presence.

IZZY: For how long? I'm not exaggerating when I say there are only a few of us left.

CHRISTIAN: It will be six months until—

EDEN: What??

CHRISTIAN: The Eastern front is one thousand kilometres away—the Soviets need to be close enough...

IZZY: You're joking. He's joking.

CHRISTIAN: They passed a motion—

EDEN: But Christian, we don't have another six weeks, let alone six months. Six months is you saying you won't fight at all.

CHRISTIAN: *They* won't, I *will*. They won't fight with the Ghetto unless they can count on the support from the Soviets. That is what the motion read, I'm sorry. But I will fight.

EDEN: I don't understand.

IZZY: I do. It's not to delay. It's a motion not to fight with us.

EDEN: I don't understand. Christian?

CHRISTIAN: It's because they think we can't win without the Soviets.

EDEN: *They?* You!

CHRISTIAN: No! Not me! I am yours!

EDEN:	You lied to us!
CHRISTIAN:	They lied to me!
EDEN:	You are them!
IZZY:	Fuck...

IZZY collapses into his cot. EDEN runs to him.

EDEN:	Izzy! He's not well.
CHRISTIAN:	Oh God... They lied to me too, Eden.
JOSHUA:	They didn't lie.
CHRISTIAN:	They did!
JOSHUA:	They are trying to do their best.
EDEN:	He has a fever.
CHRISTIAN:	I feel exactly how you feel, Eden. Damn them!
EDEN:	You are them! I trusted you. Don't touch me! Get away from Izzy. He's infectious. Don't touch us. Joshua, help me. Izzy? Is he conscious?
CHRISTIAN:	Please, Comrades.
EDEN:	Go away. Izzy, are you okay?
IZZY:	Yeah. I'm not surprised...
EDEN:	No! No doom and gloom, Isador. This is fucked.
IZZY:	I never expected it to last. Why should they die for us?
CHRISTIAN:	That's not what's happened. The PPS needs the AK right now. We don't have enough to help ourselves, let alone you, without them.

JOSHUA: We need to take some minutes. For the record.

EDEN: Fuck the minutes!

JOSHUA: This is significant.

           *They call to order. They record what has
           happened.*

           It's not antisemitism. There is an order to
           who the Nazis will kill. Jews are first. Poles
           are later. They have more time, so they don't
           want to die with us now. It's simple. Be
           it recorded. It's done and there's no more
           business for this meeting. The PPS is out of
           the coalition. We don't need to pass a motion,
           because there's nothing to vote on.

IZZY: Should we sing "Solidarity Forever"?

JOSHUA: Someone needs to alert the other cell captains.

CHRISTIAN: But I am still with this coalition. I am ZOB.

EDEN: You should leave.

CHRISTIAN: Eden, you have me. And there are others.

EDEN: How did your brother vote?

JOSHUA: Comrade Abromavitch, they want to live.

CHRISTIAN: I love you.

EDEN: Alone, you mean nothing to me.

IZZY: That isn't nice.

CHRISTIAN: I can go in the morning. But I will be back.

EDEN: No. Don't. We don't need him.

IZZY: Of course we do! You're being dramatic.

EDEN: This is very dramatic. We're fucked!

IZZY: We always were! I saw it coming with my talent for predicting the worst.

EDEN: Why aren't you too sick to talk? You'll be dead in the ground and still talking shit!

IZZY: Hey, he's the bad guy!

CHRISTIAN: I am not a bad guy!

IZZY: Nu, of course I sort of hate him. When did I not? But this is actually not his fault. I'm sure he spoke against it during the debate.

CHRISTIAN: I spoke seventeen times.

IZZY: He spoke seventeen times! Yasher koach!

EDEN: Leave.

CHRISTIAN: I'll get shot right now.

EDEN: Fine. I'll leave.

IZZY: You'll get shot.

EDEN: No, I won't.

IZZY: Yes, you will.

EDEN: I don't care. I hate you all.

IZZY: You're going to let her get shot, Dabrowski?

CHRISTIAN: What do I do?

IZZY: Stand in her way! Tackle her! Get her! She's going underneath. Dammit! She's gone.

JOSHUA: She's going to get shot.

CHRISTIAN: I know!

IZZY: Go after her!

JOSHUA: Me?

IZZY: One of you!

CHRISTIAN: I'll go.

JOSHUA: You're a smuggler. They will shoot you for sure.

IZZY: Oy God! I'll go.

               IZZY has a coughing fit halfway to the door.

CHRISTIAN: I'll go. Chaim, cover your mouth.

JOSHUA: You can't. We require you to remain alive if possible. Go in the morning.

IZZY: By then she'll be shot for sure. I can't believe you didn't tackle her!

CHRISTIAN: I can't hurt her!

IZZY: No just, like, get her. Pin her down in the middle!

               EDEN comes back into the room.

EDEN: Don't talk to me.

               She sits in the corner with her back to everyone for a beat.

CHRISTIAN: Eden...

EDEN: We're done forever.

CHRISTIAN: Okay.

IZZY: Okay?

CHRISTIAN: Honestly, Izzy. I don't need your help.

IZZY: But that's it? Work a bit hard!

CHRISTIAN: I swear, you have me. Body and soul.

IZZY: Good. More like that.

CHRISTIAN: But I will leave if you want me to. I'll respect your wishes.

IZZY: He gives up. Oy, you guys are bad at this.

EDEN: Is it my choice? If he stays or goes it's my choice, right?

JOSHUA: No. Certainly not.

IZZY: I just don't think it's wise, Eden. And you know why.

EDEN: Why?

IZZY: Because! Come on... you know why. The thing we don't mention. That thing that's so obvious, that we don't mention it? Eden's so sick, oh now Eden's so hungry...? You're going to make me mention it?

EDEN: What, do you think I'm pregnant? *(She laughs.)* Honestly boys, what a cliché. The only woman in the group is secretly pregnant? How will she protect the little baby? I'm just hungry. That's why I always take the extra bread.

                You know how we feel so smug—no, we feel betrayed even, because our people went willingly towards those trains with the promise of a loaf of bread and marmalade? Want to know the truth? Izzy had to hold me down. Right, Izzy? We were in bed together— sorry, Christian—and a kid was running from room to room talking about carts of bread in the street one over and you get the bread when you walk to the Umschlag and we knew—you told us, Joshua, that they were going to use bread to bring us to the train. We knew, and Izzy had to hold me to the bed. I bit him. I bit his arm. So, you see, Christian, I also betray, and all I want to do is survive. But still go. Come back with your charity weapons, but don't come to me anymore.

Beat.

A baby... Honestly? Maybe? But who cares?

IZZY: Fine, Christian, you're out. You don't have to ask me twice.

JOSHUA: No. Eden will stop being hysterical at some point.

EDEN: No, I won't! I mean, shut up!

A code of knocking. FELICIA is back abruptly.

FELICIA: Oh my God. I ran here.

JOSHUA: Sit.

FELICIA: I will. Oh my God. Give me that.

They pass her the potato liquor.

It's not good news.

EDEN: It can get worse?

IZZY: Of course it can.

FELICIA: Next week! God help us. They will do it next week. They will liquidate what's left of the Ghetto. It's happening next week. I ran here. My nephew told me.

CHRISTIAN: Oh my God.

FELICIA:	It's true. It's not the police coming. The SS. They will invade the Ghetto and deport every last breathing Yid. You were right. Because they cannot get us to leave, then they will come and drag us out. We have one week to prepare to fight.
IZZY:	You really are with us, aren't you, Felicia?
FELICIA:	Of course, I am! You see how I ran here? The last time I ran I was twenty. We have to get going! We don't have a choice anymore.
EDEN:	Christian has a choice. He can leave.
FELICIA:	Sure, but he won't. He adores you.
EDEN:	He's not welcome.
FELICIA:	What did I miss?
EDEN:	Tell your fucking Polish comrades that it's next week. They can watch the show...
FELICIA:	Oy vey... Did they break up? Isn't she...?
IZZY:	Shhh... I'll tell you later.
JOSHUA:	Next week. We need to convene a cross-quadrant meeting of the cell captains. Let's come to order.
FELICIA:	Yes. Now. I'm writing to the Ghetto.
IZZY:	To who? The Judenrat?
FELICIA:	No, no I'll write to the whole Ghetto. We'll paper the streets. I don't care. The whole dirty truth. Adam, the deportations, Treblinka. I'm telling everyone everything I know and I'm telling them to follow the ZOB and to fight. Because we have to get the children and their mothers and anyone else who can't fight into the tunnels. We have to get a signal to them.

IZZY:	Yes.
FELICIA:	They'll believe it from me. And if the Blue Police find me and shoot me, then that's what happens. I would be useless with a Molotov, anyway. You should see me trying to run three blocks to you here. Gottenieu!
IZZY:	You write very well, Felicia.
FELICIA:	I wrote all his speeches, you know.
IZZY:	Of course you did! Also, tomorrow we should shoot the Blue Police.
EDEN:	You're too weak. I'll do it.
IZZY:	You? It can't be a girl!
EDEN:	Are you serious?
IZZY:	I'll be fine tomorrow.
JOSHUA:	This assassination must be authorized by the joint council of the quadrants or else it won't work to signal the uprising.
IZZY:	We are the council! We are the Party!
JOSHUA:	Your hubris voice confuses me, Izzy.
IZZY:	The whole world is in this room!
JOSHUA:	We must be more organized, not less organized. Council must be called first.
IZZY:	Shoot the Blue Police tomorrow, everyone will talk. Then we drop Felicia's pamphlet. Then we shoot a German on Sunday.
EDEN:	He's right, though. Assassination without permission is not an uprising.
IZZY:	The council will get on board at some point.

EDEN: Or they will freak out at us and we'll fight and disband and be fucked. They will take time believing Felicia, too. They don't know her yet.

JOSHUA: This is a massive problem.

IZZY: Joshua, I know it makes you nervous, but everything we have ever done together made you nervous and then you do it and honestly, you are so brave. That's why I love you. We just need to do this.

JOSHUA: There is a way to do the murder tomorrow—

IZZY: Assassination.

JOSHUA: ...and not have the council disband.

EDEN: Because it will take at least 24 hours to seat the council, probably more.

JOSHUA: Without permission. Without organization. Someone, a ZOB, but a rogue actor, can shoot the Blue Police without permission tomorrow. Not you, Izzy. Someone else, with less rank.

IZZY: My Joshy will kill our first Nazi... This is why—

                   IZZY collapses.

EDEN: Izzy! Isador!

FELICIA: Put on a mask!

EDEN: He's burning. Help us!

                   FELICIA wraps a scarf around her mouth. JOSHUA and CHRISTIAN carry IZZY to the cot.

FELICIA:	Here! Let me fix his bed. He needs cold water. Where's the drinking water? Didn't you notice he had a fever?
EDEN:	He never stops talking!
FELICIA:	Please, I'm begging you all to cover your faces. I read a pamphlet.
EDEN:	I don't care.
FELICIA:	You're not the first woman to love a sick man. Get him something cold for his forehead.

EDEN tears her dress into a rag and dunks it in the water.

EDEN:	This is all the water we have.
FELICIA:	I wish it were colder.
JOSHUA:	I'll get more water.
CHRISTIAN:	Be careful. We're still under curfew.
IZZY:	I'm dying?
EDEN:	He's up!
IZZY:	I'm dying!
EDEN:	You're alive!
IZZY:	Really?
EDEN:	Shhh, just rest.
IZZY:	You don't want to hear my last words? They'll be good.
EDEN:	You're still this annoying?
FELICIA:	Keep him talking. You are very annoying, Isador!

IZZY: I think I should write a novel.

FELICIA: Bad idea.

IZZY: A novel from the perspective of the lice.

FELICIA: Just go to medical school.

IZZY: I love you so much.

                   He falls unconscious.

FELICIA: We love you too. Oy...

EDEN: What happened? Is he—?

FELICIA: He's just asleep.

EDEN: He's burning!

                   *CHRISTIAN goes to touch EDEN's
                   shoulder.*

EDEN: Don't touch me!

                   JOSHUA returns with a large pot of water.

JOSHUA: Here.

EDEN: Oh Joshy...

JOSHUA: Did he wake up?

EDEN: He was joking. He said he loves Felicia...
                   What do we do?

JOSHUA: Nothing.

CHRISTIAN: Don't say that.

JOSHUA: I can't think of anything.

FELICIA: This is what you do: You cover your mouth.
                   You bathe him like this. You pray his fever
                   breaks. Do this all night.

CHRISTIAN: I will.

JOSHUA: That's impractical. You need to leave the moment curfew breaks and you need to tell the AK and the PPS that the Ghetto will be liquidated next week and that we will need every weapon they can get for us.

CHRISTIAN: Wait for my signal. I'll meet you in the tunnels to avoid the risk of being shot.

EDEN: Like this? He's not waking up.

FELICIA: Yes.

JOSHUA: Felicia, write your letter. Eden will copy it before sunrise.

EDEN: I'm bathing him. I'm praying for his fever to break.

JOSHUA: You must copy the letter.

EDEN: You do it.

JOSHUA: No. I'm leaving.

EDEN: Why?

JOSHUA: I don't think I will be coming back.

EDEN: What? That's it? Don't you love him? He's dying, the boy that you love.

JOSHUA: I've been very happy here with him.

EDEN: If he were awake right now he would slap you.

JOSHUA: Tomorrow you need to communicate with Marek and call the council. We have one week to organize all four quadrants. You'll get it done just fine without me.

EDEN: So, you really are some kind of idiot. Someone not normal.

JOSHUA: I don't know. I guess so. I wish you understood me because, I am saying goodbye. You are my comrades.

CHRISTIAN: I understand you.

JOSHUA: Christian, along with the weapons you must bring more milk jugs from your uncle the dairy farmer.

CHRISTIAN: You have my word.

JOSHUA: Fill the milk jugs, with everything we have. Felicia, organize their burial as you planned. Goodbye.

> *JOSHUA leaves.*

CHRISTIAN: Okay. Let's get to work.

> *FELICIA and CHRISTIAN record the room and one another and then pack the recordings into the milk jugs as per JOSHUA's instruction. EDEN, throughout, is singing the traditional Jewish lullaby, "Forever Young," by Rabbi Bob Dylan, over IZZY. CHRISTIAN and FELICIA gather around IZZY as IZZY dies. The song goes too far. It borders on melodrama and it is uncomfortable. When it becomes unbearable, IZZY gets up and declines to continue.*

IZZY: I can't do this anymore.

> *The canisters are placed under the stage through the trap door.*

Epilogue

ACTOR
PLAYING IZZY: We have one more scene to perform, which is really the first scene in a new play. An epilogue set some years after the war. Christian and Joshua meet in a cafe in Warsaw. Christian, wearing a Soviet uniform of some rank, is the commander of a group of workers who must rebuild Warsaw after it was destroyed. Joshua, well dressed in a suit and aviator sunglasses, has returned to Poland from Israel on a short mission from his government.

JOSHUA enters. CHRISTIAN rises, and waves.

CHRISTIAN: Well...

JOSHUA: Comrade-Captain Dabrowski...

They shake hands.

CHRISTIAN: Please... I'm just Christian. Joshua... Thank you for meeting me.

JOSHUA: I asked you here.

CHRISTIAN: Yes, but—Anyway... Coffees? Yes. Real coffee! I'm paying.

He motions for two coffees.

JOSHUA: No no... Absolutely not. I don't even drink coffee.

CHRISTIAN: What?

JOSHUA: Why would I?

CHRISTIAN: For energy? For joy?

JOSHUA: Don't let me stop you.

CHRISTIAN: No, no… Vodka!

                Motions again for service.

                You must miss our vodka in Palestine.

JOSHUA: Israel.

CHRISTIAN: Of course! I'm sorry.

JOSHUA: No, no. I'm barely used to it myself.

CHRISTIAN: Who knows what anything is named anymore. But it's good! It's good…

JOSHUA: It is a miracle. You should come see it.

CHRISTIAN: So, here—Let me say this: I knew you would eventually seek me out and I need to apologize.

JOSHUA: No—

CHRISTIAN: Yes.

JOSHUA: That's not why I'm here.

CHRISTIAN: Please.

JOSHUA: Stop. *(Beat.)* I should congratulate you! A captain.

CHRISTIAN: A labour captain for building, that's all. Trying… We mostly dig rubble and… we tunnel actually.

JOSHUA: I learned your brother was killed. Pasha. My condolences.

CHRISTIAN: Most of the AK. Most of the PPS. Most of the Ghetto, of course.

JOSHUA: Look, let's not talk about who should feel lucky to be alive, and there's nothing to forgive.

CHRISTIAN: Can I ask you? Do you mind? How long did you wait for me in that tunnel?

JOSHUA: Not me. I was on a rooftop as a sniper.

CHRISTIAN: You survived as a sniper?

JOSHUA: I'm good at it.

CHRISTIAN: You didn't want to be.

JOSHUA: Ha. You remember. So, what happened… I had the gun. You saw that. The rifle with the missing side to the butt. Two bullets went for Lejkin, the Blue Police.

CHRISTIAN: Yes.

JOSHUA: Then there were four bullets left so I waited at some height on Mila Street and I got four SS on the first day that way. After that, everything started properly. Anyhow… I got to the sewers in time. You know how we got out. The PPS helped with that.

CHRISTIAN: I'm sorry, Joshua.

JOSHUA: Stop it. Okay—you never brought us the guns, and you never returned to fight. You knew we would fail.

CHRISTIAN: Like we failed a few months later.

JOSHUA: Yes. And then great Russia did to Warsaw what Warsaw did to the Ghetto. They left you on the inside to fight alone while they watched on the other side of the Vistula.

CHRISTIAN: Lower your voice. Here we're all Soviets now.

JOSHUA: Yes, we lost so that you could lose so that Stalin could win the war.

CHRISTIAN: Defeats on the way to victory.

JOSHUA: Our friends would be comforted.

CHRISTIAN: Listen... It would be worse if the oligarchs were allowed to rule again, I believe that. And we are building Soviet power, certainly. I'm just... One needs to occasionally remember that we are Poles, no? Or at least what has happened to us, as Poles—because we were Poles? And they don't, do they? What do you think?

JOSHUA: So, the milk jugs.

CHRISTIAN: What?

JOSHUA: I need you to dig them up. I remember some things from the map, and I've written it down. We need to find the milk jugs before the Ghetto sector is rebuilt.

CHRISTIAN: Trust me, that isn't going to happen soon.

JOSHUA: I'm leaving in three weeks, and ideally, I'll bring them with me.

CHRISTIAN: This is what you need?

JOSHUA: Yes. This is what we need from you. They are the canisters from your vegetarian uncle, remember?

CHRISTIAN: I remember. I remember every word we spoke in that crowded room...

JOSHUA: This is what we need from you.

CHRISTIAN: The letters and the papers and photographs?

JOSHUA: Yes. You have a work crew excavating around the tram station—

CHRISTIAN: No, it should be a Jew!

JOSHUA: It should. But it must be done by one who can. You.

CHRISTIAN: Wait! Where are you going in three weeks?

JOSHUA: Home, of course. I have some meetings in the west and then a ship from Marseille.

CHRISTIAN: Of course. I envy you.

JOSHUA: Listen. Comrade. We are building something properly socialist. We'll do it right. I promise. Just get me what we need, alright?

CHRISTIAN: We never got our drink!

JOSHUA: I hear poor reports of Soviet customer service.

CHRISTIAN: Embrace me instead. To the end of the war, my friend.

JOSHUA: To the end of the war.

What Happened

This is what happened: The incredibly young ZOB revolutionaries fought magnificently for weeks, longer than the armies of Poland or France fought the Nazis when they were first invaded.

When the SS realized they couldn't win in combat against their strategy and bravery, they pivoted and just lit the entire Ghetto on fire. That's how it all ended. Overwhelmingly, the Ghetto fighters died by fire, not bullets or tanks.

Despite the many volumes that have been written over the decades about the Uprising, we don't know what happened in the room portrayed in this play. We make assumptions and we take creative licence, which is always coloured by our politics and bias. Even Holocaust scholars can't claim to know what conversations transpired between people like these, and if there are any in the audience tonight, the author wants to tell you, politely, to back off. She knows she got it wrong.

We do have *The Ghetto Fights*, a military account, written by Marek Edleman, who was one of the only ZOB socialist fighters who survived the uprising. It's all of 60 pages, and it's the main source text for this play— but it's sparse.

Primo Levi wrote about how even the survivors cannot be witnesses: Only the dead know the full truth of the holocaust and the survivors try to witness on behalf of the dead. Some of the dead wrote in blood on the walls as they were being led to gas chambers: "Jews, take revenge!" An eleven-year-old child wrote in an exercise book found next to his corpse in Warsaw: "I want to be a German." Yet others collected the records of how they were living and buried them in milk canisters days before dying in their ghetto fights.

Lights fade around the open trap door where the characters buried the milk cans. The light on the trap door goes black.

End of play.

Study Guide

The supplemental material that follows was adapted from the study guide written for Great Canadian Theatre Company's premiere production of Forever Young: A Ghetto Story. *The author of the study guide is Brittany Kay. Thanks to GCTC and Ms. Kay for permission to reprint these excerpts.*

Yiddish & Hebrew Language Guide

Baruch Hashem:	Thank God
Kinderlach:	Little children, friends
Boychick:	A young boy
Girlchick:	A young girl
Goyishe / goy / goyim / goyish:	Non-Jewish
Kvetch:	To chronically complain or gripe to others over minor issues
Knucked:	Knocked together
Pesach:	Passover, a Jewish holiday
Midrash:	Stories or explanations that interpret or elaborate on the Torah's text.
Shlof:	To sleep
Shtetl:	A town or village with Jewish inhabitants, commonly found in Eastern Europe before World War II
Shep Nachas:	Derive pride or joy, especially at the achievements of one's children; congratulations

Shul:	Synagogue, Jewish holy temple
Shabbos/Shabbat:	Saturday, day of rest, often signified with lighting the candles at sundown on Friday
L'chaim:	To life, typically used in a toast
Kaddish:	Mourner's prayer for the dead
Yasher Koach:	Good job, congratulations
Oy/oy vey:	Exclamation of dismay, exasperation, or surprise
Gevalt:	An interjection of alarm
Schmuck:	Annoying, irritating person
Altekaker:	Old person, geezer
Mishugaas:	Craziness; senseless behaviour or activity
Gotenyu:	Dear god, oh my god
Breugis/Broyges:	A bitter dispute or feud (often over something minor which can no longer be recalled.)
Moshiach:	Savior, the messiah
Macher:	Influential person, fixer
Medele:	Maiden
Shoychet:	Butcher

Resistance Movements

The following are short descriptions of the resistance movements of the Warsaw Ghetto Uprising that are mentioned in *Forever Young*:

The AK:
In Polish, *Armia Krajowa*, or "Home Army." The AK was the dominant resistant movement in German-occupied Poland after 1942. It arose from the group Armed Resistance *(Zwiazek Walki Zbronjnej,)* and it absorbed most of the other Polish partisans and underground forces, growing to be one of the largest underground organizations of WWII. The AK sabotaged German supply lines, fought pitched battles against the German army, and had a leading role in the Warsaw Uprising. The relationship between the AK and Jewish groups is one of the most controversial topics in Polish-Jewish relations.

The Bund:
The General Jewish Labour Bund in Poland (known simply as the "Bund,") was a socialist organization which promoted the political, cultural, and social autonomy of Jewish workers. It was the dominant Jewish organization in Poland, and engaged in many political, educational, and social activities, including the promotion of Yiddish culture and language, and advocating for full equality for minorities. The Bund was anti-Zionist. During the German occupation, the Bund maintained connections with groups in the west and promoted solidarity with Polish workers.

Hashomer Hatzair:	Hashomer Hatzair, or The Youth Guard in Hebrew, is a secular, socialist and Zionist youth movement. Formed in the Austro-Hungarian Empire in 1913 originally through scouting programs, Hashomer Hatzair believes in the creation of a Jewish homeland in Palestine through socialist Kibbutzim. In 1939, the movement had 70,000 members worldwide. During WWII, the membership organized widespread resistant to the Nazis. The movement exists to this day.
The PPS:	The Polish Socialist Party, or *Polska Partia Socjalistyczna* in Polish. During WWII, it became an underground organization known as *Polska Partia Socjalistyczna – Wolność, Równość, Niepodległość* (PPS-WRN), or the Polish Socialist Party—Freedom, Equality, Independence. Members formed five-person cells which were under the authority of a central committee.
ZOB:	In Polish, *Żydowska Organizacja Bojowa*, or "Jewish Combat Organization." ZOB was formed in 1942, when several smaller youth groups amalgamated in order to resist mass deportations of Jews to Treblinka. The young people of the ZOB were among the first to take the threat of annihilation by the Nazis seriously.

Before Reading the Book

Exercise: Revolution and the Warsaw Ghetto Uprising

Directions:

1. Write the word REVOLUTION on the board. Elicit responses from your class on what thoughts, feelings, or examples come up when you think of this word.

2. Split students into groups and give each a piece of chart paper and markers.

3. Groups will make a three-section chart with the headings: KNOW, WANT TO KNOW, LEARNED. (KWL)

4. Ask your students to only fill in the first two sections of their chart, leaving the third (LEARNED) blank. They will fill this in after they read the play. In their KWL chart, ask students to brainstorm what they already know about the Warsaw Ghetto Uprising and what they want to know/questions they may have. If there is limited prior knowledge, you can broaden the time period by using the Holocaust as a marker.

5. After filling in the KWL chart, use the following video to foster awareness of the Uprising before reading the book: https://www.youtube.com/watch?v=fjVQgDhMuis

Debriefing Questions:

- Were you aware of this specific historical event? If not, why do you think that may be? If yes, where did you first learn about it?

- How do groups or individuals spark change?

- What makes the Warsaw Ghetto Uprising a revolution or revolt?

- Can you think of other current or past revolutions?

After Reading the Book

Exercise: Role on the Wall & KWL Chart

Directions

1. Have students rejoin their KWL groupings. Give them time to fill in the LEARNED part of their charts. Have each group share whether any of their questions were answered from reading the play.

2. On the back of their chart papers, each group will create a "Role on the Wall" character analysis for one of the five characters from the play (Eden, Izzy, Joshua, Christian, and Felicia).

3. Students will draw a generic outline of a person. On the inside of the outline, students will fill in the character's internal influences or motivations. These can be aspects such as their feelings, thoughts about themselves, likes / dislikes, personality traits, how they feel about other characters, or dreams / regrets. They can include direct lines or examples from the play. On the outside of the silhouette, students can write the external influences that affect the character. These are how other characters may think about them, societal views / pressures, life circumstances or what the character projects onto the world.

4. Upon completion, have each group present their character analysis and see if the class can add anything else.

Debriefing Questions

- How do the internal influences of these characters affect their actions or motivations in the play? Can you cite specific examples?

- In what ways are the characters' internal characteristics and external forces connected to each other? Do any of the external influences cause the characters to think differently about themselves? Can you add any additional internal ideas based on the external forces?

Exercise: Archives and Preservation

The "Oneg Shabbat" Archive, also known as the Ringelblum Archive, is one of the most impressive and unique projects initiated by the Jews during the Holocaust. This underground archive was established and run by historian and community figure Dr. Emanuel Ringelblum, with the express purpose of documenting the reality of life under Nazi occupation.

Directions

1. Invite students to research the Oneg Shabbat Archives, also known as the "milk canisters" from the play. Encourage them to find three or four actual artifacts that were buried and think about why those items were chosen. What story do these items tell? Why would they want this piece of evidence preserved?

2. If you were documenting and archiving the last two years of your life, what kinds of items would you choose for future generations to uncover? What might accurately represent your history? Students can decide between writing out their ideas or physically gathering items to present.

Debriefing Questions

- What do the Oneg Shabbat Archives tell us about Jewish life in the Warsaw Ghetto?

- What was the purpose of creating the Oneg Shabbat Archives? What were the Jewish people in Warsaw trying to do?

- In what way was the Oneg Shabbat Archives a form of resistance?

- Where are the archives today? Have all the canisters been found?

Discussion Questions

- Who writes our history? Who has the autonomy to retell history?

- Can we rely on memory alone to retell stories from the past? What is the potential danger in that? How do we preserve memory? What is the role of memory in understanding our history?

- What is Class War? Can you think of any past or current examples?

- What are the origins and history of antisemitism? How has antisemitism evolved?

- How has misinformation been used to justify antisemitic beliefs?

- Can you think of global youth groups who are clamoring for change today? What and who gets in their way?

- How do groups or individuals spark change?